The Fast-Track MI

C000115840

Co-published with Coopers an~ ~ ~~

Consultant Editors
John Kind, Director, Human Resource Consulting, Coopers and Lybrand
David Megginson, Associate Head, Sheffield Business School

THE FAST-TRACK MBA SERIES represents an innovative and refreshingly different approach to presenting core subjects in a typical MBA syllabus. The practical, action-oriented style is intended to involve the reader in self-assessment and participation.

Ideal for managers wanting to renew or develop their management capabilities, the books in THE FAST-TRACK MBA SERIES rapidly give readers a sound knowledge of all aspects of business and management that will boost self-confidence and career prospects whether they have time to take an MBA or not. For those fortunate enough to take an MBA, the Series will provide a solid grounding in the subjects to be studied.

Managers and students worldwide will find this series an exciting and challenging alternative to the usual study texts and management guides.

Titles already available in the series are:

★ *Strategic Management* (Robert Grant & James Craig)
★ *Organisational Behaviour and Design* (Barry Cushway & Derek Lodge)
★ *Problem Solving and Decision Making* (Graham Wilson)
★ *Human Resource Development* (David Megginson, Jennifer Joy-Matthews & Paul Banfield)
★ *Accounting for Managers* (Graham Mott)
★ *Human Resource Management* (Barry Cushway)
★ *Macroeconomics* (Keith Wade & Francis Breedon)
★ *Innovation and Creativity* (Jonne Ceserani & Peter Greatwood)
★ *Leadership* (Philip Sadler)
★ *Ethics in Organizations* (David J Murray)

The Series Editors

John Kind is a director in the human resource consulting practice of Coopers and Lybrand and specializes in management training. He has wide experience of designing and presenting business education programmes in various parts of the world for clients such as BAA, Bass, British Petroleum, Burmah-Castrol, DHL and Scottish Amicable Life Assurance Society. He is a visiting lecturer at Henley Management College and holds an MBA from the Manchester Business School and an honours degree in Economics from the University of Lancaster.

David Megginson is a writer and researcher on self-development and the manager as developer. He has written *A Manager's Guide to Coaching, Self-development: A Facilitator's Guide, Mentoring in Action, Human Resource Development* in the Fast-track MBA series and *The Line Manager as Developer*. He has also co-authored two major research reports – *Developing the Developers* and *Learning for Success*. He consults and researches in blue chip companies, and public and voluntary organizations. He is chairman of the European Mentoring Centre and an elected Council member of AMED, and has been Associate Head of Sheffield Business School and a National Assessor for the National Training Awards.

Coopers and Lybrand
The Coopers and Lybrand organization is one of the world's leading providers of professional services, including accountancy and auditing, tax and management consulting.

THE FAST-TRACK **MBA** SERIES

Ethics in Organizations

DAVID MURRAY

KOGAN
PAGE

Published in association with Coopers
& Lybrand

First published in 1997

Kogan Page Limited
120 Pentonville Road
London N1 9JN

© David J Murray, 1997

British Library Cataloguing in Publication Data

A CIP record for this book is available from the British Library.

ISBN 0 7494 1592 4

Typeset by JS Typesetting, Wellingborough, Northants.
Printed and bound in Great Britain by Biddles Ltd, Guildford and King's Lynn.

Contents

Acknowledgements

Since forming Maine Consulting Services in 1991, and spending much of my time researching and advising on ethical standards in business and professional life, I have been helped by many people. This book is written in my own particular style but most of the content has been learned from others, especially from client organizations in both public and private sectors, from colleagues and from the academic world.

Since 1993 I have also had the privilege of repeated visits to the post-communist countries of Central and Eastern Europe. In working with people of profound integrity struggling to come to terms with the values of a market economy and to resist what at times seems like an irresistible deluge of corruption, I have been heartened beyond words.

So many people have contributed in so many ways to this book that it must be unfair to mention only a few here, and some of the following may not appreciate just how much they have helped. To each, however, I owe a considerable debt of gratitude: Mark Bonham, Luke Bretherton, Dick Chewning, Milan Cicel, Charlie Colchester, Prabhu Guptara, the late Christine Henry, Richard Higginson, Marek Kucia, Juraj Kusnierik, Jack Mahoney, David Plater, Vinay Samuel, Peter Unwin, and Simon Webley. Also I want to thank the staff of the library at the University of Central Lancashire for their support during the period of my Visiting Fellowship at the Centre for Professional Ethics.

During the early stages of my work in this field my younger son, Nigel Murray, acted as my research assistant while at the same time working on his postgraduate studies. It was he who did most of the analysis of professional codes. Finally, my dear wife Hilda, who after 32 years of marriage still had enough patience with me not only to tolerate my ridiculous hours of work but also to read the whole of the manuscript and point out the places where I was seriously inarticulate. To her, my gratitude and love... and now we really will have that holiday.

David Murray, November 1996

1

Introduction and Overview

This introductory chapter looks first at how the book came to be written, secondly at its structure, and thirdly at its style. If, before launching into the detail, you want a mental picture of how its content will flow, what it includes and what it omits and why, as well as some insights into the standpoint from which it is written, then read this chapter. It will help you understand and benefit more fully from the three main parts that follow. You might, however, wish to go straight to Chapter 2 which outlines the first of the three parts. To obtain a quick overview of the entire book, read this introduction plus the three summary chapters (Chapters 2, 8 and 14), and finally Chapter 21 which provides some pointers for the future.

ORIGINS OF THE BOOK

One afternoon in 1990 I arrived at the New York office of the management consultancy firm in which I was then a partner. A colleague met me with the friendly interrogation: 'What are you doing here again? You seem to be more in the States than in England these days!' I told him about the two-day seminar I'd been leading on a university campus in Connecticut, and the conversation continued something like this: 'We were studying strategy *implementation*, but we started from how the personal values and aspirations of top managers influence strategy *formation*.'

His response was immediate. 'Personal values? A manager has no right to make decisions other than those which maximize value for the stockholders.' We both knew that we were using the term 'value' in very different ways. The all-too-common 1980's view of business as being primarily a vehicle for financial manipulation and the short-term enrichment of shareholders, was firmly established in the United States as well as in the UK. I could not agree with him. I can no more accept the sole right of modern shareholders than I can the mediaeval concept of the divine right of kings. Hence, years later, this book. The conversation stuck in my mind, and expanded into a repeated question, 'What is a *well-behaved business*, and what values will create it?'

Business and Beliefs

Earlier that week, in the seminar, we'd been looking at 'mission statements' and what they typically consist of. We'd seen some which focused on business objectives while others concentrated on managerial style and standards of corporate behaviour. I had been arguing that both were essential. A business which concentrates its mission statement on how it will behave, but is woolly about what it intends to achieve commercially, runs the risk of achieving very little. Conversely, an organization which focuses its mission on traditional performance objectives, to the exclusion of *how* it intends to conduct itself within its many internal and external relationships, runs the risk of becoming inhumane and socially irresponsible. Six years later I still hold to this view, which strongly informs the structure and content of this book.

MISSION Summaries: BUSINESS AND BELIEFS
(Three alternative models)

1. The mission of XYZ Transport is to become number one in both market share and profitability in our selected road transport market segments within three years, and to maintain that position while diversifying into further niches.

2. XYZ Transport aims to be the company that customers choose for its friendly and efficient response to their needs, and where its staff enjoy working.

3. XYZ Transport aims to become, and to remain, the most profitable company in its selected road transport markets by building long-term relationships between customers who enjoy doing business with us and staff who enjoy delivering an ever-improving service combined with commercial honesty and public responsibility.

In the panel opposite are three single sentence mission statements, the first emphasising business performance in traditional terms, and the second focusing on beliefs about desirable behaviour. The third combines business aims with values and beliefs, and (although it would need refining to suit any real-life business) is potentially a far more powerful instrument for managing than the other two.

Some people are unhappy with my using the word 'belief' in this context. They tend to be fairly comfortable with an external term such as 'behaviour' but uneasy with a word which digs deep inside a person's humanity, implying deep feelings and commitment. I often use the two words 'values' and 'beliefs' alternately. These are things which really matter to people, things which they believe in, principles by which they wish to live their business lives, even though conscious of frequently falling short of their highest ideals.

Questions to Ponder

Does your organization have a summary mission statement?

If so, what values does it communicate?

BUSINESS ETHICS?

According to an old joke 'business ethics' is a contradiction in terms. For some this is only humour. For others there is a serious question: 'As business is by nature unethical, how can there be such a subject as business ethics?' I will not answer in detail this assumption that business is inevitably exploitative and self-centred and in other ways immoral, except to say that in my experience it is not so. Most businesses are for most of the time managed in line with high and sincere principles of integrity. This is not to say that they never go wrong. If that were so there would be no call for this book.

Issues of morality and business can be considered at several different levels. My own preference is for the following five-level scheme, which I find to be the most practically helpful, though I often adapt it:

1. *Economic systems* (eg, *laissez-faire* market-economics; social-market economics).

2. *Organizational constitution* (eg, cooperative forms; trans-national corporations).

3. *Organizational policy and strategy* (eg, market choice and positioning; quality; environment).

4. *Functional operations* (eg, sales; finance; R&D).

5. *Individual conduct* (eg, abuse of power; whistleblowing).

I devote very little space to consideration of the ethics of macro-economic systems beyond what will be written in the next few paragraphs, and apart from a comment that not only the ethics of national economic systems but also those of the global economy need increasing attention by serious non-partisan moral thinkers. The ethical debate between liberal market and centralized command economics is outside our scope, and in any case is of decreasing relevance today. Similarly, there is little here about organizational constitution. The debate, for example, about alternative forms of enterprise ownership is not covered; you will have to look elsewhere for detailed discussion of the moral merits or otherwise of the limited liability company, or the respective virtues of employee ownership and consumer cooperatives.

Our concern here is with matters of organizational policy and strategy, with ethical issues in business functions such as marketing and personnel, and with the activities of individuals as they work in the organization. Having said this, however, a few words about *laissez-faire* economic thinking will be in order. I do not argue that everyone who believes in the virtues of free, deregulated markets and minimal legislation wishes to behave irresponsibly in society, but I am convinced that such a danger is very real.

Grapes of Freedom?

Ten years before the incident recounted above I had read two sharply contrasting books during a series of long flights, and had enjoyed them both: first Steinbeck's socially explosive novel, *Grapes of Wrath*, then Ruth and Milton Friedman's *laissez-faire* economic prescription, *Free to Choose*. Some who have read them both might wonder how I could possibly combine the two, but I did so, without imbibing undiluted the philosophy of either. I still find that life has to be lived holding apparently contradictory ideas in constructive tension.

There are conflicting views of business ethics and its twin, corporate responsibility. The 'pure' Friedmanite approach would say, 'The only way in which a business can do good is by being successful as a business, in financial terms. Its only obligations apart from those to its owners are to abide by contracts and to operate within the law. It will only do good by creating a prosperous society.' On the other hand, a multiple responsibilities approach views the positive impact of a business on human society not as secondary, an indirect concern, but as a primary obligation, and sees this as a moral issue. Within this model financial measures are by no means the only criteria against which to judge corporate performance.

We will return to this theme in Chapter 5 when we examine the 'stakeholder' model and corporate obligation. The position I adopt in this book acknowledges something of truth in both positions. Certainly in many respects a free society with prosperous businesses is able to provide a better environment for its citizens than one that is subject to over-regulation. In the latter case the blocking of initiative and drag on enterprise lead almost inevitably to reduced prosperity. Freedom is an important contributor to economic well-being.

Economic Liberty, or Licence?

Sadly, however, freedom is very easily and often abused. Liberty is frequently misconstrued as licence. The valid economic principle of self-interest all too often becomes twisted into a tortured selfishness. A society which allows its businesses to do as they will, without restraint on antisocial malpractice, runs the risk of becoming corrupt and self-destructive. To some extent legislation, regulation and enforcement are essential to restrain the worst aspects of corporate carelessness and malpractice. The ultra *laissez-faire* view insists that 'good behaviour' can only be expected of business if it is prescribed by law (and it also calls for less law). Surely it must be a morally and spiritually impoverished society which needs moral practice to be forced by statute in order to ensure decent behaviour. Does society not have the right to expect businesses to comply with basic tenets of integrity and fairness without the threat of spending a week in court?

The extreme *laissez-faire* argument fails at this point. We cannot, surely, want a society in which organizations consider themselves free to choose to operate at any level of immorality and inhumanity they please, provided that they do not break explicit laws. Nor, surely, can we wish for a society in which legislative curbs are progressively reduced to give greater and greater licence for selfish exploitation and greed by organizations which consider themselves free to do anything not clearly forbidden by those ever-reducing regulatory constraints.

A civilized economic system needs a legal framework which, while providing for initiative and enterprise, will curb the worst excesses. This, however, must be supplemented by a general acceptance among business people at all levels that many areas outside of legislative control should be policed by shared values such as integrity, fairness, honesty, stewardship, respect for human dignity and concern for others. A liberal régime is made possible only by self-control.

Organizations other than 'Business'

The title page reads 'Ethics in Organizations'. So far I've tended to refer to 'business.' Later chapters refer to issues which are relevant not only to the profit-making sectors of the economy but also to the not-for-profit sectors. While, for example, voluntary organizations and arms of government do certainly possess distinct characteristics the differences are less than is often implied. Emphasis on cold financial efficiency at the expense of humanity is not unique to the profit-making sectors, nor are such problems as racial discrimination, fraud and dishonest advertising.

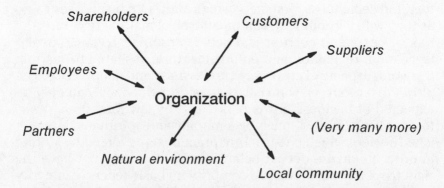

Figure 1.1 *Multiple stakeholder relationships and responsibilities*

Most managers are not 'Profit-only' people

This book is not an attack on business. It does not start from an assumption that corporate managers will inevitably do the worst that they can get away with. Rather, it starts from a view of management in which people in the upper layers of organizations are little different in terms of their moral attitudes from others in the population as a whole. The majority have no wish to preside over antisocial, inhumane or corrupt business practice. On the one hand they do not wish to be tied down by excessively restrictive legislation, and they certainly have no desire to waste valuable time navigating the complex mazes of regulatory bureaucracy. On the other hand they do want to conduct their businesses in ways which will benefit the societies of which they are a part. This book is primarily for such people. It might convince someone who is currently in the 'profit-only' school to adopt a broader, and in my view more balanced and sustainable, position but it is not primarily a tract aimed at conversion. It is designed to help those who wish to run 'well-behaved' organizations to do so, by pointing to some helpful ways of thinking about the many dimensions of the problem.

Strategic Environment or Organizational Impact?

For many years I used diagrams similar to Figure 1.1 to help me think about the environment in which a business operates. These diagrams would show the arrows pointing inwards to the company. The concern was about how the outside world was likely to affect the plans and performance of the organization.

Here now the arrows point in both directions. Not only does the business environment have its impacts (for good or ill) on the organization, but that organization makes its mark (also for good or ill) upon the environment and on its many stakeholders. One aim of this book is to help readers plan more effectively to make that a positive, and not destructive, impact.

STRUCTURE OF THE BOOK

The book is in three main parts. At the end of this chapter, and facing the first page of each of the three summary chapters, is a chart of the contents.

A Challenge to Thought

What in your view is the primary responsibility of your organization? Is it solely financial (not that profit is a bad thing in itself), to be as numerically efficient as possible in the short term? Or do you recognize a wider range of obligations, a body of stakeholders with whom you must build responsible long-term relationships? If the latter, how does your organization ensure that all these relationships are managed constructively?

Part 1 – Areas for Attention

In these chapters we will examine what it is that has made business ethics such a growth subject over recent years. We will explore a development of the 'Stakeholder' model as an aid to identifying areas for attention. After examining the rise in concern for 'values' in the business world we will look at two major areas of development which are having considerable impact on business ethics thinking: organizational complexity and change, and the transition from conducting local and national business to participating in a global economy.

Part 2 – Integrity in Action

Having explored these areas of ethical concern, and how to identify the issues in our own organizations, we take a look next at how some organizations are approaching them. Chapter 9 describes how to set about developing a corporate philosophy or a code of conduct. In Chapter 10 we examine ethical dilemmas and how to work out what to do when no solution seems satisfactory. Chapter 11 considers ethics and values programmes, and we follow this in Chapter 12 by a look at 'integrated ethical management', bringing together functions which flow naturally from a statement of values, such as safety, environmental protection, quality, personnel and customer relations. Finally for this section of the book, in Chapter 13 we consider approaches to ethical audit, performance assessment and reporting, with a few observations on recent developments in corporate governance.

Part 3 – Ideas for Progress

None of this happens in a vacuum. Organizations, whether businesses, public services, charities or anything else, are under external pressures with regard to their behaviour. There are valuable sources of help and ideas to be tapped. In fact, it will be argued that many bodies often viewed negatively as sources of untoward pressure can in fact be useful sources of help and advice. Organizations which traditionally have faced one another like gladiators (such as businesses and environmental pressure groups) may find ways to work together for the benefit of all, given a willingness on each side to try to understand the other.

PHILANTHROPY, CITIZENSHIP AND SUSTAINABILITY

It is important to differentiate between corporate ethics and corporate philanthropy. The leaders of a company may consider that it has an ethical obligation to be philanthropic (although another school of corporate ethics argues that this is 'theft from the shareholders') but for the purposes of this book philanthropic 'good neighbourliness' is for the most part outside our scope.

'Corporate social responsibility', or demonstrating good responsible 'corporate citizenship', is a vital ethical issue and will be referred to repeatedly throughout the book. It is sometimes argued that if a business-sponsored community programme, for example, gives benefit to the company as well as to the community then it is not a 'responsible' project but exploitation. Once one accepts the principle of managing for win-win stakeholder relationships, not only is it *allowable* for programmes to give benefits to both company and community, but it is highly *desirable*.

Integration and interdependency will be critical concepts in the new century. Indeed, for even a reasonable level of prosperity to be sustainable into the long-term there must be a coming together of economic, ecological, technological and human objectives. Sustainability in the sense of ensuring that anything approaching our present Western standard of living continues far into the 21st century (which I am aware is not its usual sense) demands such integration.

Demands for Altruism

'If it isn't hurting it can't be good, and therefore must be condemned', or more commonly, 'Look at XYZ company; they're making profits while claiming to be ethical; it's clearly only a ruse to make money and no genuine change of heart.'

Fortunately, most companies ignore such comments – or at least try to, although it is sometimes painful to be accused of hypocrisy in an area where one has been working hard for many years to bring about improvement. Maybe there are ethical points to be considered by the accusers themselves – such as that they may be smearing people of high principle... people with human feelings who are doing their best.

SOME ETHICAL '-OLOGIES'

The book is written as far as possible in an easily accessible style. The aim is to present up-to-date thinking but to do so in a manner which lends itself to practical application.

Each chapter contains not only an outline of major current issues and some responses to them, but also practical suggestions in the form of worksheets, checklists and models to help readers apply the ideas in real life.

In common with just about every topic of study, however, there has accumulated over the years a number of terms which, although not often used here, will be found in much ethics literature. In these final paragraphs I will refer to just four terms: deontology, teleology, utilitarianism and dilemma.

Deontology is the theory of duty or obligation. It is sometimes referred to as ethics based on the 'act' and whether or not it is 'right'. This is in marked contrast to, *teleology*, which is concerned not with an act in itself but rather with its consequences. This is sometimes referred to as 'ends-based ethics' or as 'consequentialism'. A special version of teleology is, *utilitarianism*, which is concerned to maximize 'welfare,' sometimes described simplistically as creating the greatest good for the greatest number.

There are strong advocates of each of these, and of variations on the several themes. In ordinary day-to-day practice most people when making decisions tend to combine these different approaches, although frequently without being aware of the mental processes they are using. We will not be exploring the philosophical concepts deeply, but it is helpful to be aware of whether one is thinking in terms of 'acts' or 'ends', especially when analysing a *dilemma*, which, for our purposes here we take as a situation in which all the available courses of action appear to include morally undesirable as well as morally desirable aspects. For example in order to save one life (a presumably desirable 'end') it might seem necessary to endanger another life (a presumably undesirable 'end') or to lie (in conflict with a sense of 'duty' always to 'act' truthfully). We will explore this kind of situation further in Chapter 10.

IN SUMMARY

It will by now be apparent that I am using the term 'ethics' in a fairly broad sense and am applying it quite widely. If I were asked to pick out a single idea which runs throughout the book it would be, expressed as an organizational aim:

To manage all our relationships, both internal and external, with total integrity and with a view to the long-term.

This is not offered as a definition of business ethics, but rather to indicate the territory to which moral considerations are being applied in this small volume.

Useful References

The following does not pretend to be anything like a comprehensive listing of the latest thinking on business ethics. Rather, it is a personal selection from my own library. I looked carefully over the several dozen volumes on the ethics shelves and picked out five as those which, over recent years, have been among the most helpful at various stages of my own journey into this fascinating subject.

I was tempted to rank them, but couldn't. They are presented, therefore, using the age-old compromise, alphabetical order of surname. They vary widely. Some are quite theoretical; others are practical or focus on cases. I leave you to take your pick of style.

At the ends of most of the following chapters there will be more recommendations for further reading, and in some cases references to World Wide Web addresses.

Sheena Carmichael and John Drummond (1989) *Good Business: A guide to corporate responsibility and business ethics*, Hutchinson, London.

Marie Jennings (1990) *The Guide to Good Corporate Citizenship*, Director
    Books, Cambridge.
Laura Nash (1990) *Good Intentions Aside: A manager's guide to resolving
    ethical problems*, Harvard Business School Press, Harvard, MA.
Barbara Ley Toffler (1991) *Managers Talk Ethics*, Wiley, Chichester.
Clarence C Walton (1988) *The Moral Manager*, Harper & Row, London.

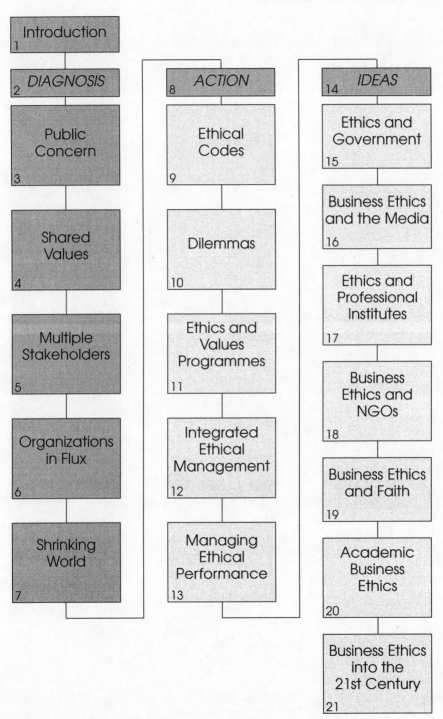

DIAGNOSIS	ACTION	IDEAS
Introduction 1		
2	8	14
Public Concern 3	Ethical Codes 9	Ethics and Government 15
Shared Values 4	Dilemmas 10	Business Ethics and the Media 16
Multiple Stakeholders 5	Ethics and Values Programmes 11	Ethics and Professional Institutes 17
Organizations in Flux 6	Integrated Ethical Management 12	Business Ethics and NGOs 18
Shrinking World 7	Managing Ethical Performance 13	Business Ethics and Faith 19
		Academic Business Ethics 20
		Business Ethics into the 21st Century 21

Part I
Areas for Attention

2

Overview of Part 1

The book is in three parts, each with a number of chapters preceded by an introduction. In working through this first part you will be helped to identify areas for attention within your own organization. Too many ethics programmes are based on generalities, on popular themes of the moment, on whatever the top management group considers to be important. These chapters challenge you to probe, and to ask yourself what are the important actual or potential weaknesses in your own particular organization. This is a vital, foundational stage in the introduction of systematic ethical management – if you really want it to make a difference. The issues are not the same in every company, in every industry, or in every country. Careful thought needs to be given by many people, in many departments, at many levels, to identifying what is important in your situation. You can use these chapters and their exercises and checklists either as an individual or in a group.

Public Concern

We start by looking at some causes in recent years of public concern about organizational behaviour. It would, of course, be doing a grave injustice to past generations to imagine that only our own has taken this topic seriously. The 19th century, while giving rise to some highly undesirable business practices, was notable also for its pioneering work in areas such as antislavery, child labour reforms, and the development of legislative frameworks to curb abuses in company financing. A society which denies credit to the ethical pioneers of the past, just because they did not address all of today's prominent themes, begins to undermine its own foundations.

Our present purpose, however, leads us to look at what is exercising the minds of the public today. We will look briefly at some of the scandals which have been influencing attitudes to business and other organizations in recent years. Even in this, however, we will turn the discussion around to direct the scrutiny at ourselves. The purpose of this is not to gloat over the weaknesses of others, but to trigger thought as to whether any of these things could happen to us.

Shared Values

As we approach the end of the 20th century and organizations face new problems, many are choosing to articulate and publicize their corporate 'values'. The aim is to enable people throughout their many departments and locations to make decisions based on common principles. This is not quite the same as having a code of conduct. Codes tend to specify behaviour in greater detail. Values, or principles, are what underlie codes. Codes can never cover every eventuality, but a set of basic values can help people make decisions in areas which the code does not touch, even new kinds of situations which have never been faced before. Values can often cross national boundaries, while rule books usually reflect closely the traditions and laws of the society in which they were initially formulated. Whereas a rule book is 'cold,' a set of shared values can generate emotional commitment to a way of thinking and working.

It is sometimes argued that there can never be consensus about values because they are so intensely personal and culture-specific. Experience shows otherwise. Worldwide, although there may be differences in detailed implementation and in the relative import-ance given to them, values such as honesty, respect for life and property, fairness and loyalty are admired and sought after. Several value sets used by others are quoted for you to consider the degree to which your own either coincide or differ. You are encouraged to begin a process of articulating your own, for your own organization, in your own words.

Multiple Stakeholders

In Chapter 5 you will be asked to think about the many relationships between your organization and others, mostly external but not forgetting those vital internal relationships such as between a business and its staff. The 'stakeholder model', although sometimes dismissed as old-fashioned or politically biased, remains the most powerful, albeit basically simple, tool to help identify the range of ethical issues facing an organization.

It is one thing, however, to list a number of relationships within which ethical issues arise. It is another matter entirely to identify what those issues actually are. At any one point in time there tends to be a number of fashionable topics, areas of alleged corporate misbehaviour and infringement of current political correctness. Fashions, however, come and go. The exercises and checklists in this chapter are designed to help readers dig much deeper than the easy headlines or the first few topics which people think to mention.

Organizations in Flux

Boris Pasternak, depicting the traumas of the 1917 Russian revolution in his book, *Doctor Zhivago*, put into the mouth of one of his characters the line: 'These men were made for times of change.' In reality, very few seem to be made like that. Although we may be reasonably capable of handling change when it happens to other people, when it affects ourselves we are less robust. Organizational change is one of the outstanding themes of the late 20th century. Everything appears to be in flux – new structures, new information flows, new pace of working, new relationships, new technologies, new business processes, new everything. Chapter 6 highlights some of the ethical issues in this complex world of change.

A Shrinking World

Jet-powered transport and satellite-supported electronic communication have effectively shrunk our globe to a fraction of its former size – at any rate for certain privileged minorities, which include potentially a high proportion of people in the Western world. The idea of the 'global village' is almost a reality. The ethical issues in this rapid and accelerating transformation are enormous. No organization can escape the implications, although many will attempt to continue living life as before. Chapter 7 examines some consequences of this globalism, and following a short discussion of the importance to major corporations of their global reputations, and a brief review of the increasingly difficult problem of worldwide software piracy, it looks in some depth at one particularly severe scourge of the international business world: bribery.

Using this Book to Practical Effect

The chapters in Part 1 may be read as free-standing entities, although they have been arranged in a deliberate sequence and you may find it helpful to follow this. You will be guided through the consideration of many challenging questions. This book is not a detached theoretical treatment of the subject. It is intended to provoke, to stimulate and to help prepare for action. Unlike many 'activist' agendas, however, it is not targeted on the real or imagined evils of others but is intended to help each of us review, self-critically, the behaviour of our own organizations.

Your Own Local Action List

It is all too easy to condemn the faults and failings of others. Major improvements in this field will come when people start to look at themselves. If you use the exercises, by the time you have finished Part 1 you will have a useful list of areas for improvement. Try talking that list through with some colleagues, select six items for attention this year – and then work to change things.

Try not to direct your mind outwards toward convenient and currently fashionable targets such as multinational corporations, road building contractors or chemical companies with manufacturing plants alongside your local river. Even when reading about some of these, try rather to focus inward on the activities of the organization in which you work, whatever kind of organization it might be. If you are a member of a crusading pressure group, ask about the standards of honesty and integrity in the conduct of its own affairs. If you are a journalist, ask yourself about the ethics of your own publication, and indeed profession. If you are a middle manager in a medium-sized business, don't even look chiefly at 'the company' but challenge your own departmental standards.

3

Public Concern

The ethics of business and organizational life have acquired a considerably higher public as well as professional profile during the past five years. At the beginning of the 1990s there were a few (a very few) conferences being held on the subject; the number of books was small; the topic received little serious attention in either management textbooks or courses; there was no major professorial chair in the subject in the UK.

All this has changed, and quite dramatically, in a short space of time. Senior managers' in-trays now receive numerous invitations to conferences, seminars and workshops on topics such as corporate values, corporate governance and other ethical aspects of management; the bookstalls carry an increasing number of specialist titles; and no self-respecting management text can now omit at least some discussion of organizational values or corporate social responsibility.

The 1980s saw a focus on rapid wealth creation, a get-rich-quick mentality, and the widespread ignoring of moral imperatives beyond P&L and cash-flow statements. We are now well into a decade of moral reflection. Business is far from being the only sphere in which this is happening, but it is particularly noticeable, arguably because of the widespread neglect of such matters for so long.

New, high-quality journals (such as *Business Ethics: A European Review*) have now sprung up. New organizations have been formed or begun to flourish for the first time, such as the European Business Ethics Network and its national subsidiaries. Consulting firms and large accountancy practices have added business ethics to their portfolio of services. Companies have sponsored market research into the ethical concerns of their customers. 'Ethical product' ranges have been developed to meet the needs of these newly identified niches. 'Ethical investment' funds have been established, investing clients' money only in companies which meet their defined criteria for corporate good behaviour. Retail customers increasingly make purchasing decisions on the basis of information about the manufacturer or distributor and its ethical policies and practices, rather than on the specification and price of the product alone.

SCANDALS

To some extent this increased interest may be a consequence of a relatively high number of widely publicized scandals. The collapse of BCCI (Bank of Credit and Commerce International), court cases following on the takeover of the Distillers group by Guinness, problems over losses at Lloyds, the Maxwell story, tales of bribery in arms procurement, and protracted confusion over the sale of arms and other strategic materials to Iraq – all contribute to a widespread feeling that there is something wrong with the moral condition of UK industry and commerce.

Europe

This is not confined to the UK. In a three-day period early in 1996 my daily press files included items from many countries. There was a row stirring over fraud in connection with European beef intervention payments in Ireland. A major German motor manu-facturer was denying accusations of industrial espionage. A European Commission official had allegedly been using his position to enrich himself. German insurance fraud was reported as being around 4 billion marks per annum. This European list could be continued much further, without even mentioning the transitional economies of Central and Eastern Europe.

The United States

In the United States a court case had finished, involving the submission of falsified quality test results on military equipment, leading to potential unreliability in life-and-death situations. A tobacco company was engaged in battle with a whistleblower who had leaked documents on the subject of nicotine addiction. Two sales representatives were being charged with defrauding a company by manipulating discount arrangements to their own advantage. The Cellular Telecommunications Industry Association (CITA) had just passed the 10,000th law enforcement officer through its training programme aimed at helping to investigate the theft of wireless services. The FBI reported that economic spying had doubled over a two-year period and that more than 800 cases were currently on the books, involving 23 different countries. According to the Internal Revenue Service there was a considerable problem with fraudulent bankruptcies in the USA, in which not all assets had been declared; the number had been estimated at around 100,000 incidents per annum and the Department of Justice had announced its intention vigorously to enforce the law.

The World Scene

On the world scene the International Monetary Fund and other agencies had been pressuring the Kenyan government to act on corruption. A government minister and several senior officials had been fired or suspended. A Brazilian bank was under investigation for having lost approaching $5 billion. The diary of an Indian businessman had led criminal investigators to a web of bribery and corruption; it was allegedly found to record his dealings as an intermediary between industrialists and politicians. The Chinese government was cracking down on corruption; imprisonments and even executions had followed. A major computer company was accused of paying kickbacks of around $21 million to win a $250 million bank contract in Uruguay.

Carried Away by Scandals?

There are several dangers in opening a book on business ethics with this kind of reporting on malpractice.

- There is a risk of exaggerating the degree to which these cases of scandal are typical of behaviour in the business world as a whole. Of course it must be true that these reported cases are only the visible tip of an iceberg of wrongdoing. It is also true, however, that the business world is a very large one, and such incidents are far from reflecting normal day-to-day life within it.

- There is also a danger of accepting at face value sensational and over-simplistic reporting. Trials, for example, tend to be reported with far greater energy when accusations are being made than when those accused are defending their reputations.

■ More serious, in terms of its impact on general standards of behaviour, is the danger that by focusing attention on large-scale wrongdoing we might lose the message that business ethics is also about the little things of life; it is not only about major crimes for which we might well deserve a period behind bars.

■ Finally, highlighting so many criminal activities associated with business and public organizations might encourage a tendency to feel that things have become so bad that little can be done to change them. We must never give way to defeatism.

Points to Ponder

Has your organization ever justifiably been the subject of unfavourable media comment on matters which you consider to have a significant ethical component?

If so, how might this situation have been avoided? What has been done to avoid repetition of something similar?

Whether or not it has happened before, how susceptible do you think you are to ethical scandals? What do you see as the ethical 'danger zones' and what should be done to eliminate the risk as far as possible?

The Public Sector

It is not only the private sector which suffers from malpractice. In many European countries, including the UK, there is a tendency to believe that private sector business behaves worse than the public sector because it is in some way less accountable to the people. This assumption frequently colours debates over privatization. It is worth remembering that the problems of alleged malpractice in ticketing on one of the soon-to-be-privatized lines of British Rail arose *before* the move from the public sector, not afterwards.

There have been many ethical challenges in the aftermath of privatising the UK's public utilities – not least questions about the appropriateness of pay levels for certain key individuals. Not only in business and former state industries but in government itself there have been highly-publicized scandals and inquiries. This experience has been shared, and even more so, by governments around Europe.

Lord Nolan was commissioned by the Prime Minister to examine standards in British public life. One of his conclusions was that it could not be said with certainty that standards of behaviour had declined. He believed that a large majority of people in public life both claim allegiance to high standards, and also largely live by them. There will, of course, always be exceptions – and the intensity of media scrutiny is greater now than it ever was. It is, therefore, necessary to strengthen provisions aimed at preventing malpractice, and to rebuild public confidence. We will examine this further in Chapter 15.

Balance and Constructive Response

Lord Nolan's observation is almost certainly relevant to most if not all sectors of the economy. Standards in most spheres of business and organizational life are probably little lower than earlier in this century. This however, is no argument for complacency. The general public does not feel this; they are bombarded with stories of bad behaviour and many believe that it is widespread and getting worse. Maybe this perception is valid. Maybe not! Maybe it was always so. This kind of argument is to miss the point. Public perception matters, even when it is misguided. Demands for improvement must meet with constructive responses. Actual standards must constantly be raised. And then the good news must be promoted to counterbalance the widespread preoccupation with things that go wrong.

THE ETHICS OF THOUGHTLESSNESS

There are many matters in the conduct of professionals not commonly dealt with by their formal codes of professional conduct but which nevertheless are of great ethical significance.

Recently I saw a letter from an estate agent to a woman approaching retirement age. She had been renting a house for the previous five months and had unfailingly paid her rent a day or two before it was due. The letter technically was only an announcement to the effect that her initial six months of rental were drawing to an end, and that she could now visit the office to confirm whether she wished to continue in the house. However, the wording of the first paragraph was in such 'formalese' that it seemed to her like an eviction notice. True, the final paragraph assured her that she could continue her tenancy, but by then the shock to her system had already been delivered!

Is this merely a trivial matter of letter-writing style? Certainly it is a matter of style, but equally certainly *it is not trivial*. It is a prime example of a professional failing to remember that the person with whom he was dealing was a human being with feelings. Legal precision does not have to be incompatible with courtesy and consideration. The fact that wording is technically defensible does not make it morally justifiable. The lack of training in how to relate to the human beings with whom they deal from day to day is itself an ethical scandal within many professions. People frequently feel attacked, insulted and demeaned by thoughtless forms and styles of expression.

THE ETHICS OF THE 'SYSTEM'

We are all familiar with the saying, 'It's more than my job's worth' – the staff member using the system as an excuse for not doing the right thing. There are also situations in which systems are designed in such a way as to benefit one side or another in a transaction. In August 1996 the BBC Radio programme, 'In the Dock' debated the public image of British banks. In a follow-up phone-in survey, 92 per cent of respondents believed that the banks did *not* serve their customers well. The reasons debated on that programme were many and varied, but consider for a moment another salutary tale – Bob's story, in the box opposite.

Bob's experience rings true to many people. I am not suggesting that banks deliberately construct their systems so as effectively to steal their customers' money for short periods. It must be asked, though, how the priorities for both bank and inter-bank system development are established. Sadly, the big financial institutions seem careless of public concern.

THE ETHICS OF POWER DIFFERENCE

This heading could take us down many avenues. I have included it as a route into considering the relationships between large companies and their smaller suppliers. This has been a matter of public debate in the UK for several years. I have myself suffered from the problem.

The Tale of the Missing Cash

Bob needed some cash. He knew that he had a healthy balance in his account. Just yesterday he'd paid several hundred pounds, all in 20 pound notes, no cheques, into his bank – or at least into a branch of his bank about 30 miles from home. Today, however, he discovered that he needed some of it – but the cash dispenser outside his own branch refused to give him anything. Why?

Inside the bank an angry Bob, conscious that ten minutes later the doors would have been closed and he would have been cashless overnight, faced a manager who seemingly couldn't understand why his customer was so annoyed. 'Yes, it will take 48 hours to register the cash paid *into* your account. Yes, cash taken *out* from a dispenser is recorded the same day. But that's just the way the system works.'

In the early years of running my own business I did a considerable amount of work for a large utility company. My fees proposal stated clearly that invoices became payable 'on presentation'. Usually that ensures payment within about a month. This company regularly took two or three months to pay. It once caused me such difficulty that I withheld *my* quarterly payment to them. Their response was to threaten discontinuation of my service. I then also issued a threat – to go to their chairman and to the press with the fact that they owed me more than 50 times what I owed them, and that they had done so for some months. After several faxes and phone calls, and considerable cost in time, I was paid. I immediately paid them.

This is far from being an unusual story, except in that I had a lever. Many smaller businesses have no leverage available to them. They simply have to suffer at the hands of large corporate bullies. Many of my readers are likely to work for large organizations. Let me ask you to consider how much of your annual bonus this year will be paid out of funds immorally withheld from small suppliers.

BUREAUCRACY – SERVICE OR CONTROL?

Style of service is a common problem with government bureau-cracies, whose staff too often appear to believe they are there to rule rather than to serve. In the UK, central government departments and agencies appear to have been improving as a consequence of Citizen's Charter initiatives, but there is still a long way to go – in both central and local government. Quality of service issues are, in the terms of this book, ethical issues. They are about treating people as significant individuals with feelings, rather than as numbers on a register.

CLARITY OF COMMUNICATION

A related topic is that of clarity. Everyone is familiar with the phenomenon of the small print at the foot or on the reverse of contracts. How often has it been used to hide away terms and conditions which might otherwise have discouraged or turned away a customer? How often has it been found to carry different legal meaning from the plain sense of the advertising blurb? How often has it been designed to confuse? Or how often has it been the product of an untidy mind hiding a chronic inability to communicate clearly with ordinary mortals behind a mask of legalese? And how often has it simply been a matter of, 'These are the words we have always used', and a failure to ask who understands them? The Plain English Campaign has been working away at this for many years now, with a large number of successful improvements in simplicity of communication for which it deserves great credit.

ETHICS AND PUBLIC CONCERN

Over the course of the past 20 years there has been an enormous increase in general public awareness of environmental issues. The highest-profile world-level event was the United Nations Conference on Environment and Development (The Earth Summit) which attracted 178 nations to Rio de Janeiro in June 1992, including over 100 heads of state. Simultaneously almost 500 groups (Non-Governmental Organizations, or NGOs) were involved in a Global Forum some miles away from the official meetings. More than any single event before or since, this summit and forum raised matters such as climate change, biodiversity and the sustainability of development to a new level in the consciousness of society around the world.

As a consequence, when starting to discuss business ethics, some people immediately assume a focus on ecological issues. Topics such as pollution, energy conservation, safe disposal of wastes and water quality are so commonly part of conversation (and increasingly of education) that ethics and the environment sometimes tend to merge. This catalogue can be supplemented by an additional list of current concerns which might include discrimination, blood sports and any form of cruelty to animals.

This book is not devoted to a narrow spectrum of issues. Certainly there are ethical concerns in all of the areas mentioned, but if an organization is to become truly ethically aware it must open its mind more broadly. There is a serious risk of organizations selecting currently fashionable issues and promoting 'ethical' products and services based on them but failing to deal with dubious policy and practice in areas unrelated to marketing advantage. Again, this book promised to be provocative. The box below contains some important questions.

Another Challenge

Does your organization market 'ethical' products? If so, how would you rate its ethical performance in other areas of organizational life, such as your personnel policies, your treatment of suppliers, and your relationships with customers? Can you lay claim to being generally (albeit not perfectly) an ethical company? Or are ethics merely a marketing ploy?

If you don't currently claim an ethical product range, but if you were to do so, what would be your priority areas for attention to ensure that this was supported by high standards *throughout* the organization?

The Inconsistency of Public Opinion

I have argued that public opinion of business and other organizations should not be ignored. That does not mean that I am falling for the deceptively clever, but utterly fallacious, proposition that perception is reality. Perceptions can be manipulated, and often are. Public opinion is often misled. It is often grossly inconsistent. In recent months public sentiment has been hot against an 'outrageous' salary paid to the head of a major utility company, and against paying Members of Parliament at such 'high' levels as to equal middle managers in not very large businesses. And yet, a football team can transfer a player in his mid-twenties to another club for a multi-million pound fee, with earnings (in salary alone, and no media complaint about other sources of income!) 20 or more times the pay of a parliamentarian. Scarcely an 'outraged' voice is heard. Consistency?

Alistair Cooke, in his weekly 'Letter from America' at the time of the Olympics, pointed out that while there are frequent complaints (and he implied quite rightly) from campaigners about the employment of small children making 'sneakers' under almost slave conditions in Third World countries, nothing at all was being said about the way in which some other countries were putting tiny children through painful training programmes to make them into world-class gymnasts.

We cannot expect public opinion to be consistent. It never will be. Neither can we afford to ignore it. The business ethics agenda will continue to be influenced heavily by it, and quite rightly. However, this should not be the end of the agenda but the beginning. Public image is important, but it is not all that matters. In our next chapter we will consider how to probe more deeply into the inner workings and relationships of your organization.

Useful References

The most useful reference source that I have found on corporate scandals is not a printed book or other document but an Internet address on the World Wide Web. I do not vouch for all of the information included either on the site itself, or on the sites to which hyper-links are provided. Many of the sites accessed from it are either official or run by professionally reputable organizations; some other items are by satirists and complainants. It has, however, provided useful sources to supplement my press-cuttings file. As when reading the newspapers, use your discretion.

The Financial Scandals Web Page http://www.ex.ac.uk/~RDavies/arian/scandals.html

Useful address: European Business Ethics Network, Nijenrode University, Straatweg 25, 3621 BG Breukelen, The Netherlands

4

Shared Values

Y ou are sitting in a comfortable armchair with a cup of coffee watching a television comedy programme. Suddenly, the screen is filled by the opening sequence of a commercial. 'Time to switch off my mind for a few minutes', you think. But then, 'What's this?' Across the screen there flashes not a fancy new motor driven by a leggy blonde, nor yet another demonstration that the nation's favourite brand of detergent is washing whiter than ever this week. No, this advert is about 'values'. An international financial services company is using its advertising budget to tell you about the principles that determine how it behaves around the world.

'Values' have become serious business. The term appears to be everywhere. Is it a sign that large organizations are thinking deeply about their standards of behaviour, about the principles that underlie the ways in which they operate? Or is it all, as some cynics would have us believe, merely another attempt to pull the wool over the eyes of a gullible public?

There can, of course, be no simple, universal answers to such questions. Without a doubt some such promotion of virtue comes merely from the creative imagination of an advertising executive. But, equally without a doubt, there is an ever-increasing number of major organizations around the world treating their corporate values very seriously indeed.

Company chairmen write about the 'core values' of their business. CEOs explain how only the existence of a body of 'shared values' enables their thousands of people to pull together toward a common goal, engaging enthusiasm and emotion as well as brain and brawn. Educationalists promote their universities on the basis of the values they espouse. Medical facilities proclaim their values of care and concern. Politicians call for a return to values of honesty, mutual concern and hard work. Media people, triggered by the latest front-page atrocity, call for values of decency and mutual respect. Values, or calls for them in their apparent absence, are all around us in the mid-1990s.

The Mars Group's Five Principles

Quality

Responsibility

Mutuality

Efficiency

Freedom

Moving from the television set to the computer screen you connect to the Internet World Wide Web. (See Chapter 16 for more Web-talk, and if this couldn't be you because you don't understand it, ask your 9-year-old son or daughter, or niece or grandchild. At that age they're all experts!) You're looking for some 'pages' on how petfood is developed. Sure enough, here it is – Pedigree petfoods, developed at Waltham – but before reaching the dogs and cats you're informed that the good people of Waltham are guided by a set of 'five principles'. What is more, these principles are not exclusive to animal lovers; they are presented as the common guides of the many thousands of people who work in the many different businesses of the Mars Group worldwide. They're even being given prominent exposure on the World Wide Web.

In the medical profession difficult decisions about patients and their families are being made on a daily basis. What principles, or guides to conduct, are available to help doctors face these often emotionally charged and distressing quandaries? Four values (nonmalfeasance, beneficence, autonomy and justice) are widely used as a set of primary points of reference by clinicians in facing

---

Four Primary Values in Medical Ethics

Do no harm (Nonmalfeasance)

Do good (Beneficence)

Respect autonomy

Ensure justice

---

these hard choices. In our work for the Institute of Health Services Management in 1993 my colleague David Plater and I suggested an extended set of primary values to assist managers in healthcare organizations. These eight working principles, in slightly adapted form, are shown in the box below.

An Extended Set of Primary Values

Do no harm	Require truthfulness
Do good	Maintain good faith
Respect autonomy	Respect the dignity of human life
Ensure justice	Seek the common good

It is sometimes argued that the effort to identify common values in a modern pluralist society is pointless, and is inappropriate for a business environment. It is argued that differences in personal viewpoint, and especially in religious background, make the task impossible. That may well prove true if one were to seek to establish common ground on *all* the values of a disparate group of people, or to attempt to give identical relative weighting to different values when facing a dilemma. Many exercises, however, have shown that it *is* possible to establish sets of 'core values' which are more than acceptable to people of different cultural and religious backgrounds. In Chapter 19, as we examine the relationship between faith and business ethics, we will look at the 1994 Code of Ethics on International Business for Christians, Muslims and Jews. Here are the four principles upon which the code was based.

Four Principles for International Business

Justice (fairness)

Mutual respect (love and consideration)

Stewardship (trusteeship)

Honesty (truthfulness)

(From: 'Code... for Christians, Muslims and Jews', 1994)

To take another example, in September 1993 a not very well known body, the Parliament of the World's Religions, met in Chicago, the attendees representing most of the world's systems of faith. As 6,500 people came together it was not, as some had feared, to work toward the establishment of a single authoritarian world religion. Among its objectives it did, however, aim to draft a basic 'global ethic' which, without falling to the level of the lowest common denominator, would be useable in promoting common standards of acceptable behaviour between people of the entire world. After considerable debate this was signed as a set of 'four commitments' (shown below; note that these were not drafted with business, economic and political organizations specifically in mind, but for general purposes). Whatever one's opinion of the value of such conferences (and opinions vary widely) it does demonstrate the possibility of gaining at least some degree of consensus on standards of behaviour among people of very different cultures and agendas.

A Global Ethic – Four Commitments

Non-violence and respect for Life

Solidarity and a just economic order

Tolerance and a life of truthfulness

Equal rights and partnership between men and women

What is a Value?

There are considerable differences of style and terminology between people working in this area. Some use the term, 'values'. Others refer to 'principles'. Some use single words; others prefer phrases or short sentences to express these ideals. Some use the various terms flexibly, others define each of them differently and keep them strictly apart. For the purposes of this book, the terms will be used flexibly: values, principles and ideals will be used as coterminous. Sometimes single words will be used, at other times phrases or sentences, and the formal definition of a 'value' adopted here is:

a sustained and deeply held preference for a mode of acting, being or achieving.

A person may, for example, wish to act with integrity, or to be free or to achieve material prosperity. Integrity, freedom and material prosperity are equally, by this definition, values.

The Value of Values

Company 'codes of ethics' come in many forms, although most are shaped around either a list of values, a list of stakeholders, or a list of potential problem situations or kinds of wrongdoing. (We will look at codes more closely in Chapter 9.) Many, however, are too much like rule books, seeking to specify standards of behaviour for almost every conceivable situation. Even when they are summarized in, say, eight statements on a single side of paper, much is lost when there is no indication of the values which underlie them. Without a set of clearly stated core values there is less to go on when a way forward has to be determined in a situation which the code drafters did not anticipate.

The inclusion of foundational values adds a great deal to the meaning of a code of ethics. For example, the statement, 'We are committed to providing superior service to our customers', can be seen to express or imply several values including competitiveness; care; promise-keeping; to name but three.

The chemicals company, Eastman, is an example of an organization which articulates its values as (almost) single words. Its 'Eastman way' contains a list of eight values – honesty and integrity; fairness; trust; teamwork; diversity; employee well-being; citizenship; winning attitude. Each of these is then elaborated in up to three short sentences.

Values and Objectives

David Packard, in his 1995 book, *The HP Way: How Bill Hewlett and I built our company*, links values and objectives very closely together. He describes how in the early days of the Hewlett-Packard Company they brought together the senior people and worked out a list of objectives. That is what they were called – objectives – but, unlike many such lists, they were heavily and explicitly value-laden. Growth was 'a measure of strength and a requirement for survival', while in discussing the products and services delivered to customers it was stressed that they should be 'useful'. Corporate citizenship was emphasized. Profit, a word much misused and abused by opponents of successful business, was 'The best single measure of our contribution to society,' to be pursued, and indeed maximized, but 'consistent with our other objectives'. Creativity, personal satisfaction, and ensuring that employees shared in the success of the company were further important components of the value mix which has been at the heart of this outstandingly successful company.

IDENTIFYING CORE VALUES

Most people, given some time for thought, can produce a list of some of the chief values which they see driving their organization. Usually, however, it becomes considerably longer than eight or ten items, which is about the limit of what can be given consistent attention by busy managers. It is necessary to identify what are the values at the heart, or the 'core' of the organization, what are the *vital values* without which serious problems will arise.

Aspiration or Actuality? An Exercise

When studying values in an organization it is important to distinguish between, on the one hand, what is *stated* by people to be most important to them and, on the other, what is actually *practised*. In one company I spent time with around 60 people, half individually and the remainder in groups, noting what they said was most important to them (for good or ill) in the way their organization currently behaved.

My list (including such topics as focusing on customers, developing people and constantly searching for ways of improving, as well as more negative issues such as a perceived culture of blame) was eventually pared down to 12 which the people involved considered to be most important. These were phrased as statements of aspiration ('This is the kind of company we would like to be'). Each member of staff was then asked to give a mark out of ten to each of the 12 aspirations. (How well do you think we're doing at present?) The distinction between aspiration and feedback highlighted many areas in which the vital values still needed to be grounded in reality. The sequence for a modified version of this exercise is itemized in the box opposite.

WHY TAKE THIS TROUBLE OVER VALUES?

My purpose in this chapter, and the whole of the first part, is to help identify areas within your organization which need attention.

Vital Values – A Practical Exercise

1. Make a list of values that you feel might be (and include some which might not be) important in your kind of organization, as far as possible keeping to single-word terms. (Here are some starters to stimulate thought: fairness; honesty; creativity; profitability; growth; determination; accuracy; compliance; patience; obedience; rationality; improvement; flexibility.)

2. Ask a group of colleagues, from a variety of backgrounds, to look at your list and to add any they think you have missed.

3. Produce copies of the list and ask each of your colleagues individually to tick the 12 they consider to be most vital to the long-term survival and success of the organization.

4. Add up the marks given to each of the items, and list approximately ten which received the most marks.

5. Discuss this list thoroughly with your group and agree a list of the organization's seven to ten most core, or vital, values with a single sentence description of each. (You may be able to take account of ideas from your earlier listings, those which didn't pass the cut, by amalgamating the sense of some of the terms into these single sentence descriptions.)

6. Give this list to a wider number of people in the organization, explaining that this is a list of aspirations, an attempt by your working group to describe how the organization would like to think of itself. Ask people to give a mark out of ten against each of the values indicating how well they think it is displayed in the real day-to-day life of the organization.

7. Based on the responses, create an action list for the next six or 12 months to improve the way the organization lives out its vital values in practice.

8. You might refine the vital values list in the light of the responses – but don't do that too often; they should be relatively stable.

These will be different from one company to another. Over-generalization is risky.

There are six main reasons given by business leaders for this kind of development. Here are the first two:

- *The business benefit* – 'We need something to create a unity in our organization, so that we can compete to best advantage; without shared values we'll not create maximum value for shareholders.'

- *The right thing* – 'We want to build an organization with true integrity, not only one that does the right thing in the sense of obeying laws, but one that provides a quality of working life for its people and satisfaction for its customers by doing what is right, consistently; this is how things ought to be.'

The first person here could be described as the economic pragmatist, the second as the moral crusader. For the second, ethics and values are ends in themselves. For the first person they are secondary, in that they contribute to the achievement of something else, the maximization of shareholder wealth, which appears to be seen as the ultimate value; some advocates of the first position see moral values as primary in other areas of life, but only as secondary once they reach the office.

In practice the two are often combined, on the argument that when an organization does maintain high ethical standards and lives up to its declared values this is also good for business. Two Fortune 500 companies are worthy of quoting on this theme. The final paragraph of the Johnson & Johnson 'Credo' puts it very clearly, after discussing obligations to customers, users of their products, employees and society at large: 'Our final responsibility is to our stockholders... When we operate according to these principles, the stockholders should realize a fair return.' The ServiceMaster Company, after an emphasis on people ('the dignity, self-respect and worth of each individual') continues, 'Many companies view profit as their sole reason for existence, and indeed it is necessary for business survival. At ServiceMaster, profitability is not an end in itself, but rather a means of accomplishing our other objectives. ...Profitability is a way to test and challenge ourselves.'

Four further reasons for emphasizing values are often quoted:

- *Changing attitudes/aspirations* – there is in Western society a widespread move toward people wishing to live their lives as consistent 'wholes' rather than in compartments. Many people are less and less willing to leave their personal values behind them when they arrive at the office or workshop. The concept of an ethically distinct world of work, where different values hold sway, is increasingly unacceptable to many people. Organizations will have to come to terms with this. The drive to values may well come from the 'coalface' as well as from the boardroom.

■ *Changing patterns of work* – as a greater proportion of the working population works with the mind rather than with the hand, as the number and variety of 'professional' jobs increases and the proportion of educated and articulate people rises, pressures will be brought to bear on many companies from the inside to change their value systems, including areas where blue-collar employees were often unable to have any substantial influence.

■ *Positive encouragement* rather than negative prohibition – there is today a tendency for many people to resent 'Thou shalt not' morality. Organizations will need to maintain their rule books of what is and is not permissible, especially where legal compliance is the issue. Values development, however, enables management to focus on positive messages of improvement, which are much more affirming and empowering than prohibitions.

■ *An urgent need for values education* – in many Western countries, as the traditional foundations of moral education and standards are being removed, increasing numbers of younger people appear to have rejected, or even be unaware of, the basic codes that make a civilized society sustainable. Some industrialists believe that schools, churches and families have failed in this, and that there will be an increasing educational role for business to play with respect to literacy, numeracy and standards of behaviour. Otherwise many in the rising generation, especially but not only in cities, will be incapable of working constructively with others.

This last point may seem at first sight to contradict the earlier points. Just as Western society becomes more polarized in terms of wealth and poverty, so it is with values. The challenge of building organizations with anything like homogeneous values is likely to increase for many years to come.

Will any values do?

I have stressed the need for organizations to articulate their own sets of values. Does it make no difference what those values are? I believe that it matters greatly! An organization that develops a set of values incorporating deception of customers, dishonest and self-centred aggressive competitiveness between colleagues, and carelessness toward the environment would clearly be unacceptable to anyone not aiming to undermine civilized society. Foundational principles such as honesty, fairness, trust and respect for human dignity may be phrased differently to make them relevant to individual organizations, but are essential to a sustainable human society and must be present in some form.

Useful References

Tom Chappell (1993) *The Soul of a Business: Managing for profit and the common good*, Bantam Books, New York.

Hans Küng and Karl-Josef Kuschel (1993) *A Global Ethic*, SCM, London.

Ronnie Lessem (1990) *Managing Corporate Culture*, Gower, Aldershot.

Paul McDonald and Jeffrey Gandz (1992) 'Getting Value from Shared Values', *Organizational Dynamics*, Winter, pp 64–77.

David Packard (1995) *The HP Way*, HarperCollins, London.

Edgar Schein (1985) *Organizational Culture and Leadership*, Jossey-Bass, San Francisco, CA.

Mike Woodcock and Dave Francis (1989) *Clarifying Organizational Values*, Gower, Aldershot.

5

Multiple Stakeholders

I t was pointed out in Chapter 1 that the stakeholder model in business ethics inverts the reasoning of the old-style corporate planner's scanning of the business environment. The organization now asks not only, 'What effect will these have on us?' but also, 'What impact will we have on these?'

Integrated Performance Measurement

Only a few years ago this was relatively rare thinking. In the UK it has received considerable reinforcement from the adoption of stakeholder logic by the 'Tomorrow's Company' inquiry of the Royal Society of Arts, from 1993 to 1995. Within their model, the 'Inclusive approach to sustainable success,' they emphasize the multiplicity of relationships within which companies will need to manage and measure performance if they are to retain society's long-term 'licence to operate'.

Others have also been advocating a broader base of performance measures. Robert S Kaplan and David P Norton publicized their 'Balanced scorecard' method in two highly regarded papers in the *Harvard Business Review*. They take four perspectives: financial, customer, internal business, and innovation and learning. Using a model which is worthy of an examination far more thorough than we have space for here, they talk in terms of creating value along all these dimensions.

Assessment for the Malcolm Baldrige quality award, which is possibly the highest prestige corporate award in the United States, goes further. It includes the examination of performance under two main heads, 'enablers' and 'results', the potential marks being split 50/50 between the two. An economic or industrial traditionalist might expect to find the 'results' described in terms of measures such as profit, cash-flow, liquidity and long-term increase in shareholder value. Certainly these are included, but such 'business results' account for only 30 per cent of the total possible results marking. The other 70 per cent of outputs are listed under the headings, 'People satisfaction', 'Customer satisfaction', and 'Impact on society'. Neither the RSA nor the Baldrige model considers an organization to be high-performing if its performance is 'high' only in financial terms for the benefit of the shareholders while the interests of other stakeholders are being ignored.

There is some distance still to go, however. At present in these models, although such factors as impact on society are considered in the scoring, they still tend to be viewed as somewhat distinct from 'business' performance. Managers using the models, while valuing the 'non-business' output measures, can still hold them in their minds as separate add-ons. We now, however, *may* be seeing a gradual, and hopefully irreversible, trend toward business performance being measured in a comprehensive and fully integrated manner.

Is 'Stakeholder-thinking' Legal?

One common response to arguments like those above is that the directors of a company are under a legal obligation to work to increase the wealth of the shareholders, and that therefore to take more than passing account of 'these other interests' will land the directors in trouble with the law. This is not the kind of book in which to attempt authoritative legal opinion, but increasingly this objection is considered not to be sustainable, on at least two grounds. First, at least under English law, directors are obliged to promote the interests of the company. Shareholders constitute only a part of the company as a whole, and in any case the particular set of people and institutions who happen to hold shares on any one particular day are not the shareholders as envisaged by the law. Shareholders in general and into the future must be taken into account.

The second argument is that it can scarcely be in the interests of the company, or even of the shareholders in particular, to put the future prosperity of the organization at risk. What could be more risky, in terms of longer-term societal opinion, than managing the business in a biased manner, in the interests of only certain interested parties and with only a limited number of performance measures permitted to influence decision-making?

STAKEHOLDERS – WHO ARE THEY?

The stakeholder model calls for each organization to think carefully about the many different constituencies upon which its activities and performance have an impact. Each will, in detail, identify a different list, but for the business community generally the following are among the most commonly considered:

Customers   Employees
Suppliers   Regulators and legislators
Local communities   Natural environment
Owners   Financial institutions
Competitors   Strategic partners

These can often be broken down further into subgroups, but the important point is not so much the detail or the precision of the analysis as the honest consideration of what are the ethical issues in the organization's relationships with each.

Figure 5.1   *Stakeholders; similar to Figue 1.1, showing different interests*

How are your employees treated? As human individuals, with personal worth, or as anonymous numbers in a tightly-controlled headcount? How are your suppliers treated? With honesty, toughly in negotiation, but fairly? Or as people to be pressurized, manipulated, bullied and exploited until they continue to do business with you solely because they can't afford to do otherwise? How do you relate to your competitors? Do you think in terms of vicious warfare, and act accordingly? Do you steal their secrets and slander their reputations?

These are issues for all organizations. Every board and management team should spend time on this, considering what standards of behaviour they should be aiming for, and how (in down-to-earth practical terms) they are going to make any needed improvements. Some of the items will already be dealt with under headings such as health and safety, equal opportunities, internal

---

Customers are Stakeholders

'Customer care' has been a popular theme for several years. Have you asked yourself recently:

■ Do we keep our promises to customers, or do we make promises that we know we can't keep?

■ Are we honest about the quality and prices of our products/services?

■ Do we respond helpfully when a customer complains?

■ Do we think of the customer's inconvenience when we fail to deliver?

■ Are we working to build long-term mutually advantageous (win-win) relationships with customers?

■ Would I like to be one of my customers?

No doubt you can think of other similar questions. Keep on asking and answering them – honestly and seriously – then do something about the answers; promote the good points, and correct the bad.

---

audit and customer service. Others may be covered as yet by no explicit policy or action programme. They cannot be ignored in the longer term without putting society's licence to operate at some degree of risk. This chapter incorporates several boxes containing challenging questions. You might also consider devising your own sets of provocative questions – to include stakeholder groups and topics which are not mentioned here but which are relevant to your organization.

Suppliers are Stakeholders

The most efficient organizations treat their suppliers (and in turn their customers) as partners in a joint enterprise. This does not imply the end of tough negotiation, but it does mean that the outcome of negotiations should be to the long-term benefit of all parties. The following questions will help you start an appraisal of your supplier relationships:

■ Are you honest in negotiating with your suppliers?

■ Do you pay your suppliers on time in accordance with your agreements?

■ In dealing with businesses much smaller than your own, do you bully, and abuse your power?

■ Do you ever either offer or accept bribes?

■ Do you behave toward your suppliers as you would like your customers to behave toward you?

Long-term trusting relationships up and down the supply chain help build stable businesses.

STAKEHOLDER ISSUES IN DIFFERENT FUNCTIONS

Each specialist function within an organization gives rise to its own areas of ethical concern. Each has its own variety of relationships to manage. The first two 'challenge boxes' raise relationship questions with respect to customers and suppliers. While of relevance to the organization as a whole they will be of particular interest to departments such as marketing, sales and purchasing. Within each department, however, the really important stakeholder issues are likely to be at finer levels of detail than these inevitably broad-brush questions. We will look at some such specific points in just two functions.

Finance

The finance function is one in which major issues of probity arise. These concern not only legality and illegality but also shadow-lands such as those in which the financial condition of the

Stakeholders – Society and Law

In societies where there has been democratic rule of law for many generations one can expect that overall, with occasional exceptional inequities, legislation and taxation structures will be accepted by the majority of the people. Where such institutions are newly emerging the situation can be far more complex – with laws which are inadequate or even contradictory, taxes which are penal in their nature and levels, and administrative bureaucracies which are either incompetent or corrupt or both. Wherever you live, try challenging yourself with the following questions:

■ Do you comply with legislation and regulations affecting your kind of business?

■ Do you provide honest information to the authorities when required?

■ Do you seek to avoid tax, as distinct from seeking to minimize it within the law?

■ If the system penalizes honest business, or is corrupt, what are you doing within your constitutional framework to help improve it?

organization is publicly reported, where the true situation can be considerably camouflaged without breaking the law. Terry Smith's book, *Accounting for Growth*, highlighted many of the techniques in common use for deliberately masking difficulties and enhancing the apparent prospects of a business. In Chapter 1 we looked at different approaches to ethics. An 'act' may be totally legal, but it is important to ask the question, without either oversimplifying or over-generalizing, whether intent and 'consequence' make that act ethically supportable.

Information Technology

Information technology is another functional specialism in which considerable attention is now being given to ethical questions. Computer science, information processing and communication

The Natural Environment as a Stakeholder

All the other 'stakeholders' in this model are human. The environment is different in this respect, but nevertheless should be treated as a genuine stakeholder. Future generations will be affected for good or ill by how we treat the natural resources entrusted to us. Here are some searching questions:

■ How much waste material is generated by your business? What are you doing to reduce it?

■ Do your processes cause atmospheric pollution? If so, do you have a plan to eliminate it?

■ How much energy (light and heat especially) is wasted in your business?

■ Do you take note of suppliers' environmental performance, and favour those acting responsibly?

■ Have you applied the principles of environmentally sustainable economics to your plans?

technologies have been driving fundamental and accelerating changes to working life and to entire societies. No longer can it be considered acceptable to change simply because it is possible to change. The impact of major technological developments, and of the associated transition processes, contain major ethical components which can no longer be downplayed as they often have been in the past. Society will ultimately hold the technology, its developers and its implementers to account for problems in such areas as:

■ impact on human relationships

■ data integrity and security

■ access, power and disenfranchisement

■ reduced relevance of geographic location.

This last point gives rise to a range of complex moral questions about, for example, the desirability of moving an accounts processing office to the opposite side of the globe because (at least in the short-term) it is cheaper to employ Indian staff than

Employees are Stakeholders

Employees are the heart, the mind and the muscle of a business. Too often they are treated merely as mechanical arms and legs. Most 'stakeholders' are external; here is an internal group with a profound interest in the conduct and performance of the business. The employer or manager who treats them merely as bodies and brains bought to obey without thought or feeling, is living in the dark ages. Can you answer yes to the following?

- Are you honest with people when you employ them, about the business and about their prospects?

- Do you pay people fairly – relative to one another and to others outside?

- Do you treat your employees as human individuals, and encourage their development?

- Do you keep to both verbal and written contracts, and not cheat employees when it suits you?

- Do you protect their health, safety and security against potential hazards in your business?

European. Until recently such decisions were mostly made with regard to an organization's physical production activities; now they must also be made in relation to administrative and knowledge-based work.

STAKEHOLDER ISSUES IN DIFFERENT BUSINESS SITUATIONS

Different business situations give rise to different ethical challenges. An organization going through a period of major growth will face different quandaries from one experiencing the painful process of structural contraction in its industry. One expanding within a familiar culture will probably have fewer dilemmas to resolve than one entering several new and unfamiliar markets around the world. This will be the case especially where business customs and practices in the unfamiliar markets include activities which would be condemned as unethical by professional codes and possibly also by legislation in the home country.

Local Communities are Stakeholders

For each local community in which your business operates, ask yourself the following questions then devise four more questions for yourself:

- Does the appearance of your premises make this a more or less pleasant area in which to live?

- Do your processes put local people at risk?

- Are there local amenity projects with which you could help, possibly cooperating with others?

- If there is high youth unemployment locally, is there any way you could train a young person?

- Could you provide useful paid work for a handicapped person?

This is not to suggest that time and money be spent on major community activities to the extent that the business itself deteriorates. That would be seriously counter-productive for all concerned. But it is worth asking yourself periodically, 'Is my company a good local citizen?'

It might be assumed that the moral dilemmas of contraction would be greater in both number and difficulty than those of expansion, but this is not necessarily the case. Contraction may incorporate highly visible moral pressures such as those associated with redundancy decisions and severance terms, but the apparent successfulness of expansion frequently masks tensions. Relocation decisions, long working hours, tiredness, irritability leading to blame and fear, strife within marriages and families due to pressure of work – these and more can be the consequences of a business seeming to go well. Another common problem of growth is the allocation of recognition and reward for the success, which is rarely simple (see Chapter 13).

Any significant change in an organization affects a large number of people. It is good practice, as part of the implementation planning of a change programme, to carry out a stakeholder analysis, to ask who will be affected either directly or indirectly, in what ways to what degrees – and then to consider the plan for

Competitors are also Stakeholders

In many stakeholder models competitors are excluded. They are frequently thought of more as the enemy. Many books have been written advocating 'warfare' strategies. Sometimes it is even suggested that anything other than such confrontation is contrary to the basic principles of a market economy.

- Do you ever lie to your customers in order to damage competitors?

- Do you steal competitive information, such as by espionage methods or by deliberately recruiting their staff in order to obtain secrets?

- Does your advertising insult competitors rather than promote honestly your own competence?

- Do you ignore the patent rights, trademarks and other intellectual property rights of competitors?

- Do you ever pay bribes in order to gain a competitive advantage?

Honest competition, in which businesses vie with one another to attract and retain customers by meeting their needs better than any other organization, is a vital foundation stone of a market economy. A culture of warfare, however, will lead sooner or later to abuse and even to criminality.

change in the light of your organization's values (Chapter 4) and code of conduct (Chapter 9).

STAKEHOLDER ISSUES AT DIFFERENT ORGANIZATIONAL LEVELS

Much of the formal thinking about ethical issues in organizations tends to take place toward the top, either at the rather rarefied level of the board, or by groups of senior managers and functional specialists. Possibly this is the reason why some 'Code of conduct' documents seem theoretical and remote from the real day-to-day life of staff.

As will be discussed in Chapter 11, an ethics programme needs to involve people from all levels. The chairman may be concerned about the principles underlying top-level corporate reporting. The quality inspector, though, is more likely to be worried about the consequences of his having last week given way to pressure to falsify a test record, or the secretary to be angry at having been instructed to lie about the date on which a letter was received.

In the first chapter I suggested four levels at which business ethics can be studied within an individual organization – plus a top level, the national/international economic system. Here I add a layer. These levels are not absolute. You may wish to develop your own layering, appropriate to your own particular type, size and complexity of organization. The vertically expanded model can be summarized as:

- *Governance* – responsibility to owners and the community.

- *Direction* – planning and steering the strategic way forward.

- *Allocation* – allocating resources; controlling performance.

- *Supervision* – ensuring agreed quality, time and cost.

- *Operation* – making product; providing service and support.

This kind of model can be useful in analysing, clarifying and simplifying hierarchical structures. It also helps as a framework within which to identify the different kinds of ethical pressure at different organizational levels in relationships with different stakeholders.

Not only does the mix of stakeholders vary between levels of an organization, but so does the nature of the relationships.

A chief chemist's participation in national committees to establish the next generation of pollutant emission tolerances involves different kinds of ethical question from those faced by his plant technician struggling manfully to prevent a toxic spill reaching the nearby river, without sufficient protective clothing for the staff working on it.

If a stakeholder analysis is to be meaningful to people at all levels in an organization, it needs to be studied at all levels – and communicated in terms of relationships which exist at these many levels.

STAKEHOLDER ISSUES IN DIFFERENT INDUSTRIES

In some staff support areas the kinds of ethical issues raised, and the stakeholders involved, are broadly similar from industry to industry; this goes especially for such functions as personnel and finance. On the other hand, those functions closer to the core of the business vary considerably. When carrying out a stakeholder analysis one should consider what issues and relationships arise from the nature of the product or service, from the characteristics of the customers served, from the model of ownership and organization (for example, the mutual constitution of a building society versus the corporate constitution of a bank), from the technologies used, and from geographical and cultural diversity.

REFLECTION

1. What are the seven principal stakeholder relationships of your organization – taking account of its scale and complexity, its geographical spread, its customer mix, its technology and its industry sector?

2. How do those stakeholder relationships manifest themselves in *your job*? Are any of them of lesser importance in your position? Are there others which take precedence in your particular sphere of work? Make a list for your job of around eight relationships.

3. What ethical issues tend to arise in each of the relationships you have listed?

4. How do you normally know, or sense, that things are going well (or badly) in the relationships that you have listed?

In some sectors there are few distinctives; in others these industry-specific issues will be the outstanding features of the analysis, such as in healthcare, in education, and indeed in any 'industry' concerned with intervention in the lives of people.

Stakeholder Planning

There is no need to make this complicated. Many businesses fail in new initiatives when they introduce unnecessary complexity. Plan to treat your stakeholders well by following this simple sequence.

1. List your stakeholders, starting with those mentioned in this chapter but remembering that you may have others, or the categories suggested in this chapter may be too broad and need splitting into subgroups.

2. Working with other people in your business, list against each type of stakeholder (a) the ways in which you believe you currently treat them well, and (b) the ethical problem areas you can see in the relationships.

3. Annotate your list with notes as to the *causes* of poor stakeholder relationships, and also of good, ethical relationships.

4. Convert your list into *action* points, things you're going to do in order to build further on the things you're doing well or to correct the problems; set completion dates for the most important.

5. Against each action point list one or more measures, or indicators, which will enable you to know and to demonstrate to others that improvements are being achieved.

6. Identify what needs to be done by *other people*; agree actions with them, including for each item a date and basis for reviewing progress.

7. If you already have a business plan for the year ahead, add these actions to the programme.

8. Consider how you might convert each point into an opportunity, to differentiate your business and to attract and keep customers.

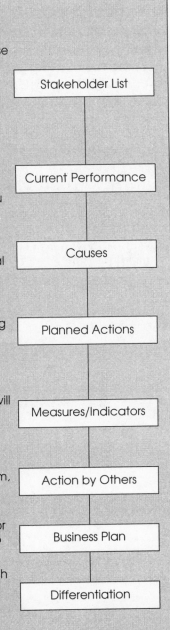

Stakeholder List

Current Performance

Causes

Planned Actions

Measures/Indicators

Action by Others

Business Plan

Differentiation

USING THE MODEL

The stakeholder model, with its many possible degrees and directions of extension, provides a powerful starting point for many ethics programmes. It can help examine the impact of a profession on many areas of society, en route to developing a professional code of conduct. It can form a helpful early stage in identifying the critical relationships of a company or department. It can be the starting point for an ethical risk analysis. Indeed, it is possibly the most powerful tool in the diagnostic toolkit, especially if used in the multidimensional way outlined in this chapter.

Useful References

Charles Handy (1993) 'What is a Company For?' *Corporate Governance: An International Review*, vol 1 no 1, January.

Robert S Kaplan and David P Norton (1992–3) *Harvard Business Review*, Jan–Feb 1992, 71–9 and Sept–Oct 1993, 134–47.

RSA (1995) *Tomorrow's Company: The Role of Business in a Changing World*, Final report, June.

Terry Smith (1992) *Accounting for Growth: Stripping the Camouflage from Company Accounts*, Century, New York.

6

Organizations in Flux

Having spent the best part of 20 years helping companies and governmental institutions to restructure and change their ways of working, I am not about to challenge the necessity of organizational change. Businesses and other bodies must continually adapt to take account of factors such as shifting strategic priorities, developing technologies, new patterns of competition, and changing economic environments.

I have, however, during those years observed that much change is handled in a less than ethically commendable manner. This is not chiefly because those responsible deliberately intend to behave immorally. It is due more to the ethical components of change management not having received sufficient exposure and debate. In this short chapter some of the issues are raised. As with other topics covered in the book, no easy generalizations are offered. The point is not to state categorically that certain things are either right or wrong, but to stimulate moral reflection.

CHANGE IS EVERYWHERE

Change is all around us. This is a truism; in a very real sense it has always been the case. As we reach the closing years of the century, however, the pace appears to be hotting up. What are the drivers of this accelerating change, especially in the business world? In the late 1980s and early 1990s many organizations which had grown fat and slow sought to recover their lost efficiency and effectiveness. This brought about many major corporate slimming exercises. Now, as we move into the late 1990s the slimming continues and will without doubt continue to do so for some years, but there are in addition other forces driving change. Two major themes are:

- The impact of new technologies, especially in communications.
- The increasing competitiveness of developing countries.

The first drives organizational change from the inside as radically new organizational forms become possible; the second drives it from the outside as vigorous, thrusting new competitors, especially from around the Pacific Rim, seek to attract business away from Western organizations.

Improve or Die

No organization can escape the fact that its competitors are getting better. Very few of the leading companies of 20 years ago, in almost any sector, are still the leading companies today. In simple terms, the company which does not improve continually, both in small incremental steps and also by leaps of innovation, will inevitably decline and die. It will end up offering the market what it no longer wants, or will offer it at levels of price and quality which are unsustainable in contrast to the competition. Time will become in more industries what it already is in many: the key factor in competition – not only timely delivery but minimum time from concept to market, and this not only for designs using familiar technology but also for innovative products incorporating untried technology which must nevertheless be reliable.

Reflection

1. What major changes have there been in your organisation during the past five years?
2. What forces have been driving these changes?
3. What ethical issues do you now feel arise from the way in which change is managed?

Benchmarking exercises increasingly enable companies to compare their performance against world-class competition using a wide variety of both internal (process) and external (visible results) indicators. These must drive continual change if companies are to thrive. Jobs are changing rapidly. Commentators such as Robert B Reich see the development of a fundamentally different mix of employment types within the economy of the early 21st century. In Chapter 14 of his book, *The Work of Nations*, he outlines three categories of job, each described as service: routine production services; in-person services; and symbolic-analytic services. He describes the radically different set of skills and the new approaches to education needed to prepare people for symbolic-analyst roles, identifying, solving and brokering problems by manipulating abstract symbols. Other futurists talk similarly in terms of knowledge-workers in an information economy.

It is possible that yet other developments will give the pace of change still another boost. Biotechnologies may revolutionize the whole of life within a few years, or it may take several decades. This is not yet clear. Social movements such as the dramatic rise in ecological awareness may possibly stimulate substantial change across many areas of economic life, within shorter timescales than presently expected as the unsustainability of current economic systems and behaviour becomes more apparent.

Moral Implications of Radical Change

Whichever drivers predominate in the future there can be no doubt that accelerating change is with us for some time to come. With some technological developments there are immediately apparent ethical issues. Expert panels have for some years been examining the ethics surrounding developments in such fields as genetic manipulation. The pros and cons of the genetic screening of applicants for insurance policies are being debated. Much heat is being generated around questions of control over pornographic content on the Internet, which is an issue not only for parents but also for companies providing access even where they play no part in creating or storing such content. We will return to some of these points in the final chapter as we look forward into the 21st century.

As to those developments which lead to organizational change, they may be exciting to some, but will become increasingly terrifying to those less well-equipped, either intellectually or psychologically, to cope. Many will fall by the wayside, either because they are genuinely not capable of learning new skills and developing new attitudes, or more likely because they are demoralized and afraid, incapacitated by (often unwarranted) feelings of failure and inadequacy.

Managers responsible for the major transitions ahead of us must prepare for the moral challenges involved. They must be willing to take into account the human issues involved in economic, technological and organizational change. They must be prepared to help people come to terms with transition, and to build new relationships in new ways in new organizations, serving new markets with new products and new services. It will not be acceptable merely to claim that everyone's future is his or her own responsibility and to throw on the human scrap-heap people who have devoted 20 years and more of their lives to their organizations. Managers with highly developed, multifaceted leadership skills must be capable of strengthening others to say farewell to the familiar past (sometimes almost equivalent to a bereavement) and of inspiring them to welcome the exciting unfamiliarity of the future. If this sounds exaggerated, it is possibly because it is understated. The managerial challenges will be enormous.

A Macroeconomic and Geopolitical Parallel

Think of the transitions taking place at present in the former communist countries of Central and Eastern Europe. Although in certain respects some of these national transitions are proving successful this is in many places at enormous human cost. The sudden removal of social safety nets in the name of free market economics has left millions in despair. Rigid control of money supply in some countries has left workers without wages for months at a time. Economists without a factor in their equations to take account of the demands of humanity have pressed politicians into imposing agony on millions in the name of freedom.

True, it is not so serious as was the conversion in the opposite direction during the 1930s when, hidden from the rest of the world, millions died of starvation during the changeover to collective agriculture, but the pain is real and severe nevertheless. The conversion to market economics was and remains essential for the long-term good of all the people, but the full consequences of the moral insensitivities of the transition-engineers have yet to become clear. In some places return to a totalitarianism of some kind may well yet be the result, and all the pain will have been for nothing.

It may be that Western societies will prove capable of taking care of the physical needs of people during their less traumatic economic changes, but for many this will not reduce the emotional pain. Moral issues must come higher on the agenda if the challenges are to be faced successfully. This is not only a requirement for building prosperous businesses into the future, but for securing the stability of society.

If the above paragraphs seem to paint rather a bleak picture, it is not an inevitable one. Change can be managed successfully, and must be! Most of us can start to learn by taking ethical issues into account in the smaller-scale changes that we have to handle all the time, and in the types of organizational review projects which are commonly being implemented at present.

ETHICS AND ORGANIZATION REVIEW

In recent years we have seen a steady stream of new terms coming into the organizational change vocabulary: downsizing; rightsizing; business process re-engineering; delayering; the virtual organization; outsourcing. Each of these has its prophets and has its rightful place in the armoury of the 'compleat professional'. Each has benefits to offer, in its right place, but serious problems arise when the latest popular tools are used inappropriately.

Choosing an Approach to Change

Here is a first moral issue: the criteria by which the approach to change is selected. Too often it appears to be on the basis of the consultant's slick tongue (and I write as a consultant) or a desire to copy someone else's success formula rather than on a rigorous assessment of the need in its unique context. Delayering has seemed to many companies a neat and easy route to salary cost savings; by definition, once the prophets had declared the over-flabbiness of traditional bureaucracies, jobs in the middle had to go. But what happened later?

Consider the banks. More than one discovered to its horror when the economy turned down that it no longer had an adequate supply of branch managers with experience of managing lending through a recession. They'd disposed of their experience base by choosing an approach to cost saving which was inappropriate. As a consequence the organization, its shareholders, its customers, not to mention the pensioned-off managers, all suffered.

The Ethics of Techniques

Then there are moral issues in the way reviews are conducted. Consider the development of business process re-engineering. A powerful tool for increasing an organization's performance, if only it had taken account of the critical role of interpersonal relationships in the flow of processes, it came to be dominated by calculators and mechanistic flow charts. Then again, once a review is under way, how rarely is it abandoned even when grave suspicions about its usefulness begin to surface. How many consultants being paid for a 'down-sizing' have had the courage to stand firm against the client and insist that in some areas at least the 'right size' calls for an *increase* in staffing rather than a decrease. No doubt it has happened, but how often?

Change?

1. Which of the tools and techniques of organisational change have you been involved with in recent years?

2. How were these selected for use, and how applied?

3. How were the findings implemented?

4. What moral lessons were learned from the experiences?

5. What steps have been taken to avoid the mistakes in future, and to gain from the positive lessons learned?

Management by fad is not only unprofitable, it is unethical. In Chapter 4 we discussed the importance of corporate values, and you were recommended to list your organization's vital values. If the principles of good stewardship and of creativity featured in your list (either in those words or similar) then managing by taking uncoordinated doses of 'managerial magic potions' will certainly fall foul of them, and probably of several more on your list. If this paragraph seems rather insulting toward top managers then it is written more in sorrow than from any other motive. Having been a management consultant since the late 1970s I have repeatedly experienced (and still do) the problem of clients wanting standardized prescriptions, which they 'know' will work because they have been used elsewhere!

Ethics and Implementation

Over the years I have seen a number of excellent examples of how to implement major change. The well-being of the people involved has been at the head of the management agenda, especially when redundancies have been unavoidable. Sadly, this has not been universal. I well remember on a hot Friday afternoon being taken on one side by the leader of a staff team with whom I (as their external consultant) had been working closely, early and late, for several months on a restructuring exercise. 'I'm sorry', she said, 'I won't be seeing you next week; I've just been told to pack my things and not to return on Monday – after 15 years here!'

Reorganizations certainly are often necessary, and some of them will inevitably be painful, but when their changes have been decided on, too many companies fail to take into account the human aspects of the implementation. It is possible to organize support for people going through the transition, and it is possible to avoid appearances of gross inequity – especially general perceptions that top managers are receiving inordinate rewards for firing large numbers of junior staff.

Outsourcing of services has become fashionable, and in many cases quite appropriately. This often means that staff who once worked for the company will in future be employed by a newly appointed external contractor. The more enlightened organizations take the trouble, and consider it their duty, to check on how the new, more economical, contracting firms treat their staff. Unfortunately, many have not. Following many a downsizing or outsourcing the victims have struggled to survive on greatly reduced pay, or queued in employment exchanges while their former directors have banked large bonuses as reward for their 'achievement' of financial efficiency.

NON-STRUCTURAL ISSUES

The changes referred to in the above paragraphs have been changes of structure and of organizational size. In parallel, many other kinds of change have been taking place in the way that organizations are managed and people are developed. Two can be mentioned here.

Ethics and Empowerment

For many decades the management literature has contained articles with titles such as, 'Delegation and how to do it.' Sadly, the art and science of effective delegation does not seem to have become particularly widespread in that time. One still hears the same tales of domineering managers who hold all the power to themselves and rarely let a significant decision be made by a subordinate.

Recently the terminology has been changing. Instead of delegation we now hear talk of 'Empowerment'. Actually, in the minds of many it means the same as delegation, but not always! To an increasing number of people it means something much more. It means an attack on the very concept of authority and hierarchy, at least until the existing authority structure is removed... and replaced by a new one, which for a time has to be operated in a somewhat different style but is no less authoritarian. There is a need for considerably more research in this area, not only into the abuse of hierarchical power but also into the abuse of its removal and replacement.

Ethics and Personal Development

Another widespread concern relates to the manner in which psychologically questionable methods are sometimes employed within development programmes to manipulate both individuals and groups, frequently supported by the argument that new ways of thinking will be needed in future and that new paradigms must be developed on non-rational bases.

The Association for Management Education and Development in 1993 devised and issued an 'Ethical Charter for Manager and Organization Development'. One of the concerns highlighted during that exercise was the use, even by large and usually responsible organizations, of manipulation techniques based on pop-psychology, some of which were potentially damaging, and often without participants being informed of what was being done to them. The charter calls upon AMED members to,

> Ensure that their clients and all those participating in any process know what will be involved (given that detailed information may be inappropriate in some cases) and have given their informed consent before the process commences [and to] take account of the rights, needs, pressures and problems of others and seek to avoid asking others to do things which offend their conscience.

THE CHALLENGE

Change will not go away. It would be highly undesirable for it to do so. There is so much in every area of life to be improved.

However, if the transitions to a 21st century sustainable society are to be handled successfully (in terms of minimizing damage to the people who are negatively affected by them) then considerably more attention needs to be devoted to:

- Selecting the methods to be used in devising options for change.

- Applying these in a truly professional manner.

- Choosing the way forward, based on sound ethical criteria.

- Implementing change with humanity.

Well in advance of planning for specific changes companies should be preparing their people for the future. An idea in vogue at present is that people should be responsible for their own development. There is a great deal of wisdom in this, in that it creates a sense of personal responsibility but, sadly, some firms interpret it as meaning that they themselves need not invest in their people's futures. Nothing could be further from the truth. If an organization is to sustain its effectiveness and prosperity into the future it must develop the capabilities of its people, and those capabilities must include the capacity to absorb change.

Reflection

What am I doing to prepare my staff to be capable of handling significant change, even though I don't and can't know what it will consist of or when it will come?

Going beyond the development of individuals, leaders in many organizations are now looking into what is needed to become genuine *learning organizations*. They are concerned to discover how their organization, viewed as a body with many parts, can learn from its environment and its collective experience and so adapt successfully to the changing world. Given the pace and acceleration of continuing change such a capacity will become critical. Ethics come into this in at least two respects. First, collective learning should in itself be seen as an ethical issue, being fundamental to the very survival of the organization. Second, that organizational learning needs to include learning about processes of ethical reflection and decision making, as being themselves principal areas for development and improvement.

Useful References

The following refer to the subject of economic and organizational change, but include little on the subject of ethics. The reason is that there is as yet a serious shortage of quality work on the ethical issues involved in organizational change, although Peter Senge covers some important values in Part IV of his book listed below. These volumes are suggested as helpful in triggering reflection.

Tony Grundy (1994) *Strategic Learning in Action*, McGraw-Hill, Maidenhead.

Jon R Katzenbach, *et al* (1996) *Real Change Leaders*, Nicholas Brealey, London. (This is the output of a long-term study of organizational change by a team at McKinsey & Company.)

Ronnie Lessem (1993) *Business as a Learning Community*, McGraw-Hill, Maidenhead.

Robert B Reich (1991) *The Work of Nations*, Simon & Schuster, Hemel Hempstead.

Peter Senge (1990) *The Fifth Discipline*, Doubleday, New York.

Business Ethics in a Shrinking World

The world is getting smaller. There has, of course, been international trade for thousands of years, but distances were long and travel was slow. The development of faster ocean transport, both wind- and steam-powered, opened up immensely greater possibilities to the 19th century international businessman. The coming of transoceanic flight had an even greater impact on the speed of events, and meanwhile the invention of cable and wireless telegraphy and the international telephone call made communication almost immediate, at least for verbal conversation. Satellite communication added volume and quality. The miracle of television added an immediacy of visual image and now, with computer networks spanning the globe via the telephone system, for much of business it matters little whether an office is next door or on the opposite side of the globe; information is available at the touch of a button.

Products are conceived in one country, designed in another, manufactured in a third using components from half a dozen others, and sold worldwide. Companies exist with revenues exceeding the entire national economy of many countries. Relationships between organizations and individuals in different countries are not only those of supplier and customer and competitor, but of ownership and partnership and alliance, of adviser and facilitator.

Many commentators, such as Robert Reich (formerly of Harvard University, and now US Secretary of Labor) and Kenichi Ohmae (the former head of McKinsey & Company in Japan) are convinced that the process of globalization has gone so far that the very idea of a national economy is obsolete. Reich stresses the global economy; Ohmae a small number of regional blocs, but on this they are agreed: the days of managing any significant business within the boundaries of a single nation-state are past. From all sides organizations are called upon repeatedly to become 'world-class' – although precisely what this means and implies is frequently left unclear.

What does all of this signify for our subject of business ethics? What new issues are brought to the fore? One thing is certain; people from different cultural and religious backgrounds are having to work together in constructive and harmonious partnerships as never before. Mutual trust is having to be developed between people who still do not understand one another's patterns of thought.

Ethics and Etiquette

It is important to distinguish between ethics and etiquette. The two are often confused. It used to be said, for example, that it was unethical for a member of a profession, such as an accountant or a lawyer, to advertise his or her services. There still are major ethical questions to be asked about some of the more aggressive forms of business development, such as the common American practice of 'ambulance chasing' in which clients are signed up by lawyers when under considerable stress and in no condition to make rational decisions. Whilst, however, it may be possible to advertise in ways which are unethical, it is very difficult to sustain the argument that *by definition* all advertising, ie, making potential clients aware of one's existence and capabilities, is unethical. This is now generally recognized, as is the fact that the erstwhile ban on advertising was more one of 'gentlemanly courtesy,' of traditional etiquette, rather than one of morality.

To take another example, in the UK it is not accepted practice, and is firmly frowned upon by the system, for an individual patient to make a direct approach to a hospital-based consultant. Sometimes it is said to be 'unethical' – all approaches for service must be made via reference from one's general medical practitioner. There are certainly some ethical components to this convention, such as avoiding the risk of wasting the senior specialist's scarce time on matters which could easily be dealt with elsewhere, and consequently taking her attention away from more needy cases. For the most part, however, the matter appears to be one of administrative convenience and of etiquette based on long tradition.

As one moves into the international sphere such matters become even more important. Learning and taking great care over many aspects of courtesy, common practice and etiquette can be critical to building good relationships with people of a different culture. Initially most people in all countries will be tolerantly, if sometimes condescendingly, amused at the failure of the uncouth foreigner to come to terms with correct style. Eventually, however, that period of amusement runs out, and turns to annoyance at the apparent arrogance involved in a 'refusal' to act correctly. The primary ethical issue is often less to do with the national or local practices themselves than it is with treating people respectfully and with consideration as equal human beings. Those of us from Western cultures are often the worst offenders in this regard.

GLOBAL BUSINESS ETHICS

The ethical problems most commonly faced vary from one part of the world to another. Lists of principal moral concerns tend to be similar from country to country and from continent to continent. Differences tend to be more matters of the relative weighting of issues, and of seriousness in the public mind at a particular time. Some of my own work in Central and Eastern Europe, reported jointly with Dr Marek Kucia, identified a number of moral issues most commonly considered as serious by business people in Poland and Slovakia. The lists could almost have been produced in the UK. The differences are about the relative intensity and therefore priority of the problems.

Many people consider the quest for a global set of ethical principles for business to be rather like searching for the end of the rainbow. And yet, much progress has been made in recent years. Later in this chapter, and again later in the book, we will look at the Interfaith Declaration and the Code of Ethics on International Business developed by a group of eminent Muslims, Christians, and Jews encouraged by HRH the Duke of Edinburgh, HRH Crown Prince El Hassan Bin Talal of Jordan, and Sir Evelyn de Rothschild.

Once the external, presentational differences of etiquette are penetrated, a considerable degree of commonality lies at the heart of the matter. This is not to claim that *practice* is the same from country to country, or from culture to culture. Nor is it to say that the *relative importance* accorded to different moral ideals is uniform across all societies. Indeed, differences in the resolution of moral dilemmas can be very different between, on the one hand, societies which emphasize the significance of the individual and, on the other, those which lay greater stress on community. In one society, for example, truth may be valued above loyalty; in another, loyalty may come before truth. Each society might value both truth and loyalty very highly, but when the two come into conflict in a dilemma situation a different one might most commonly win.

GLOBAL AWARENESS – GLOBAL REPUTATION

One of the major changes in the past decade has been a rapid increase in general public awareness of what is happening in other parts of the world. This frequently includes the activities of business organizations as well as pop-stars and politicians. No company can be confident any longer of hiding misbehaviour behind the mask of distance.

This net also catches companies which have handled complex dilemmas thoroughly and responsibly but have arrived at difficult decisions with which single issue campaigners disagree. All too often public awareness and opinion is biased by the need of the media to run circulation- and audience-building stories. Companies must learn to be more effective in protecting their reputations.

No company can afford to ignore the experience of Shell with the decisions over decommissioning and disposal of the Brent Spar oil storage buoy. This was a complicated matter, over-simplified by banner headlines and distorted by single-issue bias. It included complex dilemma decisions, within which assessment of the alternative courses of action called for intensive study, profound technical understanding and great wisdom. There were no obvious and easy answers available. WWF-UK (the World Wide Fund for Nature) has since done a great service to education by developing, with the assistance of both Shell and Greenpeace, a computer-supported teaching pack for schools. This, in a non-partisan manner, exposes students to the difficulties involved and the lack of simple solutions. Meanwhile, Shell was exposed to negative international media coverage in many countries and suffered especially seriously in their Central European markets.

Whether one looks at the use of timbers from the Amazon rain forests, allegations of 'slave' labour in the prison system of China, or the payment of fair prices to coffee growers, activities which once were invisible, several steps back in the supply chain from the end-user, are now considerably more visible. Consumers increasingly are taking what they view as moral performance into account when buying many products. Companies cannot afford any longer to dismiss this as the agitation of a few extreme activists, but need to protect their reputations by effective external promotion where they have a genuinely defensible case, by rapid positive action where they don't, and by internal programmes to ensure that there are fewer 'nasties' hidden away waiting to be uncovered by activists or investigative reporters (who are often, though not always, anti-industry in attitude).

SOFTWARE PIRACY – A GLOBAL PROBLEM

Many of the ethical issues in international business might seem to the average manager or staff member to be far removed from their level of operation. As the information age becomes a reality around more of the globe there are some matters which come very close to each one of us. One of these is software theft or, as it is sometimes called, 'software piracy'. According to research carried out by Spikes Cavell & Co. for Microsoft in early 1995, more than 80 per cent of software in use in Germany, Italy and Spain (to choose just three European countries) has been illegally copied. In Japan, they report, the figure is 90 per cent.

Much software can now be downloaded from bulletin boards and the Internet, either as demonstration versions or as shareware (which is no longer 'cheap and cheerful' but now includes some very sophisticated packages). Files can easily be transmitted between machines via modem to the opposite end of the earth.

Challenge

How much unlicensed software ('pirated' – ie, stolen) do you have in your department? If none, congratulations.

The use of software in many locations, on even more machines, for the cost of only one licence (if that) is a common practice which costs the software industry literally billions of dollars each year. It exposes many managers to legal penalties including, in some countries, imprisonment. Internal software auditing is now becoming a significant requirement in large organizations, many of which are put at serious financial risk by the unauthorized copying activities of their staff, including the application of 'unofficial policies' by information technology departments seeking to make more of their budgets than they can morally or legally carry. Following the research mentioned above, Microsoft issued a comprehensive advisory and support package under the name LegalWare, not only to reduce the frequency of theft but also to manage better the total software asset of an organization.

It is very difficult to be precise about the level of piracy, and the figures quoted above are just one set of estimates. Other organizations, such as the Business Software Alliance of Washington, DC, have been monitoring trends for almost a decade – and they are worsening. In 1995 they estimated the average rate of piracy across 25 European countries as 58 per cent, with figures ranging from 35 per cent (Switzerland) and 43 per cent (Finland and the UK) to 91 per cent in Poland and 95 per cent in Romania. BSA's figures for Germany (50 per cent) may be considerably less than those of Spikes Cavell, and it may well be true that these figures almost pale into insignificance by comparison with South America, but none of this negates the overall argument of both organizations that software theft is a major economic problem.

In a paper at the ETHICOMP95 conference in Leicester in March 1995 a Polish speaker (A Kocikowski) challenged BSA's numbers for his country as being overestimates, but confirmed that in spite of there now being copyright legislation in place there is indeed a problem, especially in the private sector. He also highlighted another related question, that of software pricing. When a common word-processing or spreadsheet package costs the equivalent of six weeks average pay it seems inevitable that there will be a strong temptation to use pirate copies. Without seeking to justify this, and without minimizing the practical difficulties, there may be ethical considerations for the software companies themselves in terms of establishing more equitable price equivalence from country to country.

It is something which affects organizations of all sizes. Indeed, small organizations may be at even greater risk due to buying machines carrying pre-loaded software packages without licences. Even in a small business that, in addition to major software, uses a number of shareware packages, I find it advisable to check periodically whether I have remembered to pay the shareware fee for everything that I have continued to use after the expiry of its free trial period.

CORRUPTION – BRIBERY AND EXTORTION

Bribery is another aspect of international business which unfortunately it is difficult to avoid. I think it was an Australian journalist who first said that following the autocrat, the bureaucrat and the technocrat comes the 'kleptocrat' – the man (or woman) who steals from the less fortunate by the indirect means of receiving corrupt payments, and then maintains power by use of the wealth so acquired.

In spite of the economic, political, social, moral and spiritual damage caused by bribery it is not universally condemned. Many excuses are made for it by people who:

- have a personal interest in the system and are seeking to salve their consciences, or

- believe that it would be wrong in a modern enlightened age to seek to impose 'Western' values on the cultural mores of other parts of the world, or

- believe that business ethics should remain at a rarefied theoretical level and avoid disturbing anyone's actual behaviour, or

- are unaware of the serious economic and moral damage that corruption is causing to individuals and to entire societies around the world, or

- are prepared to look down on countries where corruption is rampant and say, 'Well, that's how they do things there; we have no choice.'

We are also often informed that there is so much corruption in countries such as the USA, Britain, France, Italy and Germany that we of the West have no right to complain at its existence elsewhere. We are told that bribery does no harm, that it fulfils a positive economic role by 'lubricating' the wheels of commerce, and that the wealth 'trickles down' to the poor also.

Another Pause for Thought

How often do you hear morally suspect behaviour justified by, 'Everybody does it'?

Does your organization follow the rule, 'When in Rome, do as the Romans do'?

This last idea must seem rather peculiar to the people of, say, the Philippines, a country among the ten poorest in the world but whose late president was among the ten richest individuals in the world. Sadly, it is true that there is corruption in the Western democracies, but in most it is noticeable for its exceptional, highly-publicized outbursts rather than for being endemic throughout society. As to being an accepted part of the local culture in many countries, if this is true how can one explain the rapid increase in major anti-corruption campaigns which are taking place at present (1996) on every continent, and from grassroots to presidential palaces, and its almost universal illegality and undercover nature? Corruption:

- Distorts decisions in favour of those who can pay.

- Further enriches the already better-off, holding the poor down in their impoverishment.

- Rewards those who are dishonest and greedy.

- Leads to unnecessary purchases of products and projects, using up scarce resources which could have been put to better use, international aid programmes being particularly suscept-ible to this kind of problem.

- Results in super-luxury projects where something basic would be more appropriate.

- Leads to products being supplied, and projects being carried out, by organizations less competent than those which would win the business under fair competition.

Bribery

A model sentence for a corporate code of conduct:

The offer, payment, demand or acceptance of bribes in any shape or form, in any circumstance, is totally unacceptable in this organization; discovery will be followed by severe disciplinary, and possibly legal, action.

Western observers sometimes claim that bribery is part of the accepted way of life in the Islamic world. It is true, of course, that some Muslim countries do have unfortunate reputations in this respect, but so also do some countries with centuries of Christian tradition. It is ludicrous to suggest that one faith or another permits it. Where it exists it is the consequence of disobeying the principles of the faith, not of following them. Bribery is condemned from all sides. The Code of Ethics on International Business for Christians, Muslims and Jews, quoted at greater length in Chapter 19, insists that companies shall 'not tolerate any form of bribery, extortion or other corrupt or corrupting practices in business dealings', and goes further in its section on suppliers when it calls on companies to 'require buyers to report offers of gifts or favours of unusual size or questionable purpose.'

The Caux Principles, developed by an international group of business leaders, state categorically, under the heading, 'Avoidance of illicit operations': 'A business should not participate in or condone bribery, money laundering, or other corrupt practices: indeed, it should seek co-operation with others to eliminate them.'

John T Noonan, a judge of the United States Court of Appeals, in his book, *Bribes*, which is probably the most comprehensive history of bribery ever written, after almost 800 pages of detailed analysis and argument highlights four reasons (shown in the box here) why bribery is 'likely to continue to be morally condemned' in spite of the many arguments made for its more liberal treatment.

Many international businesses now include in codes of conduct issued to all staff a clause similar to that in the box on page 82.

Noonan's four reasons

Why bribery is likely to continue to be morally condemned:

1. Bribery is universally shameful.
2. Bribery is a sell-out to the rich.
3. Bribery is a betrayal of trust.
4. Bribery violates a divine paradigm.

PETTY CORRUPTION – WHAT CAN BE DONE?

In considering action against corruption one must distinguish between levels. Petty corruption is endemic in very many countries, which is a different thing from the 'grand corruption' so common in international 'Aid' programmes and the armaments industry.

In many post-communist countries, for example, a person might bring along a gift to the doctor's consulting room in order to be seen by a well-qualified professional who is paid so little that she needs these extras to help keep her family. The owner of a new small business might have to build into his start-up budget a 'commission' to get a telephone line installed in less than 18 months; there's nothing in the price list to say this, but without it little will happen but delay, delay and more delay.

This kind of corruption is no less damaging within a society than the large-scale payment of millions into Swiss bank accounts to lubricate the political wheels and obtain the contract to build an unnecessary airfield or harbour jetty. The remedies, however, will be different – and may take considerably longer. In many countries where petty corruption is rampant, public officials at middle and junior levels have great difficulty in supporting their families on their extremely low salaries, and in many places even those low salaries may not have been paid for several months.

Action

When preparing people for overseas business travel does your organization provide briefing/training on important points of general and business etiquette in the countries to be visited?

Do you have a code of conduct dealing explicitly with the question of bribery? Is it widely circulated? Are all your people involved in overseas business aware of its contents? Is training provided on how to apply it in practice?

Have you worked out your marketing and selling strategies and tactics for 'difficult' countries with the problem of bribery specifically in mind, so that your people have powerful and attractive business propositions to offer which are clean?

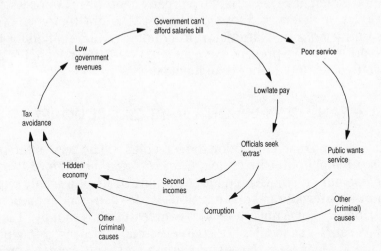

Figure 7.1 *The vicious cycle of petty corruption*

The introduction of realistic pay scales for public officials (backed up by the assurance that they will be paid on time) would make a substantial difference. Many officials practise extortion not because they wish to do so, but because it seems to be their only way of surviving. However, for governments to be able to pay their salary bills they must first receive their tax revenues. This means that the populace as a whole must pay its taxes. Figure 7.1 above illustrates some of the elements of this complex vicious cycle.

A 'business integrity' research programme with which I have been involved during recent years has received similar comments repeatedly in countries throughout Central and Eastern Europe. One of the greatest difficulties that we experienced in getting the programme started in Poland was a widespread fear that we might be investigating surreptitiously on behalf of the tax authorities. Bulgarians and Hungarians, Romanians and Slovaks, have all observed that taxation is seen in very much the same light as the spoils taken by past foreign conquerors; it is therefore to many minds an honourable thing, almost a patriotic duty, to avoid paying.

Quite apart, therefore, from elements of criminality such as Mafia-type protection rackets and other violent extortion, the reduction of petty bureaucratic corruption calls for attention to multiple components of a complex system. Changing attitudes to taxation which have been built over many centuries of oppression by foreign invaders and foreign ideologies is not the work of a year, or even of a decade. Major programmes will be called for to re-position and re-present governments and their agencies as servants of society rather than its masters.

GRAND CORRUPTION – WHAT CAN BE DONE?

At the level of grand corruption the remedies will be very different. In his privately published book, *Grand Corruption in Third World Development* (1993), George Moody-Stuart deals powerfully with this topic. International organizations issue their condemnations of bribery; government leaders investigate (usually their predecessors') scandals, fire civil servants, and send a few old men to jail. Meanwhile the offshore numbered bank accounts grow fat.

Moody-Stuart insists that the cure must be in the wealthy 'North' nations, rather than in the impoverished third-world countries of the 'South'. He identifies 'just two elements' as essential:

■ Establishing that it is as unethical – and if possible as illegal – for a company (or an individual) from the North to give a bribe in order to obtain business in the South as it would be in its (or his) own country, and

■ Making it impossible for chairmen and directors (including non-executive directors) to ignore the possibility that the company for which they are responsible is indulging in grand corruption.

He continues by recommending that a clear distinction be drawn between business gifts at a 'reasonable' level and corrupt inducements, suggesting a maximum of 2 per cent of contract value or $100,000, whichever is the lesser of the two. He calls for additional audit certificates indicating consultancy fees ('or any similar euphemisms') paid in connection with the obtaining of contracts, and for an annual chairman's declaration explicitly stating that he or she has enquired within the organization and that corrupt payments have not been made.

Whether or not the adjustment upwards of senior official and ministerial salaries in developing countries would make any significant difference is a matter of considerable disagreement. On balance, I believe that the amounts potentially available to people at these levels from corrupt practices are so great that no increase in salary or other official rewards could suffice to make a change. The action must come from the advanced countries and from international financial institutions and aid agencies.

What an individual can get away with depends substantially on his or her nationality. The Foreign Corrupt Practices Act certainly puts a brake on bribery by US organizations, although no one would claim that it stops it totally. In most 'North' countries, however, the law allows companies to escape prosecution for corruption overseas, even where the same act committed at home would lead to severe penalties. In certain countries the legislative framework is even more lenient, corrupt payments overseas being eligible for tax relief back home.

International Action

As this book has been in process of writing during 1996 there have been several developments on the international front. The International Chamber of Commerce (ICC), founded in 1919, is possibly the world's largest business organization, bringing together businesses and business associations in more than 130 countries. It has been updating its 'Rules of conduct' with respect to 'Extortion and bribery in international business transactions'. The revision is significantly more demanding than its predecessor. The 1977 version forbade bribery aimed at obtaining and retaining business. The 1996 version forbids bribery *for any purpose*.

The new ICC rules commit the organization to promoting its application throughout the countries in which it operates, and to developing processes for monitoring developments and providing advice. It also calls on governments and international agencies such as the World Bank to take action against corruption, and includes in this appeal the OECD which in 1994 issued a 'Recommendation' to member governments on the subject. Since the ICC rules were published the OECD has taken another step, by confirming its recommendation at ministerial level, stressing the need for action to achieve greater international uniformity in both the tax deductibility of bribes and the criminalization of bribery.

Transparency International (TI) is a German-based worldwide anti-corruption lobbying organization with chapters in more than 30 countries around the world. It has argued persuasively that (non-retrospective) anti-corruption legislation should be introduced throughout the European Community. It is extremely important for legislative action to be taken on a broadly similar

TRANSPARENCY INTERNATIONAL STANDARDS OF CONDUCT

Transparency International's Standards of Conduct reflect the conviction that large-scale corruption subverts economic and social development. TI is a coalition of governments, private sector participants and international aid and financing agencies, designed to counter corruption in international business transactions. These Standards apply to the coalition partners and take account of past initiatives by such organizations as the International Chamber of Commerce and the United Nations.

Article I: Respect for laws and standards

All parties to international business transactions should respect and conform to all relevant laws and regulations and to observe the letter and spirit of these Standards.

Article II: Improper inducements

1.   No party to an international business transaction should request, demand, offer or make a gift in any form, or extend any other advantage to or for the benefit of any public official or as he or she may direct (and whether directly or indirectly) as an inducement for action or inaction by the official.

2.   All parties should take measures reasonably within their power to ensure that no part of any payment made in connection with an international business transaction is received directly or indirectly by or for the benefit of a public official with decision-making responsibility or influence, or of their relatives or business associates.

3.   All parties should take measures reasonably within their power to ensure that subcontracts and purchase orders relating to an international business transaction are not used as a device to channel payments or other benefits directly or indirectly to or for the personal benefit of public

officials with decision-making responsibility or influence, or of their relatives or business associates.

Article III: Agents and consultants

1.   All parties should take measures reasonably within their power to ensure that any commission or remuneration paid to any agent, consultant or other intermediary represents no more than appropriate compensation for legitimate services; and that no part of any such payment is passed on by an agent, consultant or other intermediary as an improper inducement in contravention of these Standards.

2.   All parties should take appropriate measures to ensure that agents, consultants and other intermediaries are not employed to gain any improper influence in connection with obtaining or retaining any business.

Article IV: Financial disclosure

All parties should maintain accounting systems in accordance with best international accounting practice under which all financial transactions are properly and fairly recorded in appropriate books of account available for inspection by boards of directors, auditors and other authorized persons. In this context there should be no 'off the books' or secret accounts, or any documents issued which do not properly and fairly record the transactions to which they relate.

Article V: Political contributions

Contributions to political parties or committees or to individual politicians (or to other persons or entities at their direction) should only be made or solicited in accordance with the applicable national law, and all requirements for public disclosure of such contributions should be complied with fully and promptly. Even where permitted, they should not be made in circumstances where, given their magnitude or timing, they could reasonably be construed as exercising undue influence aimed at securing a special advantage with respect to an international business transaction.

Article VI: Definitions

These Standards should be construed widely and in accordance with their spirit. In particular the expression 'all parties' includes national governments; national and international agencies involved in international lending and aid-granting activities; corporations and other enterprises involved in international business transactions of all kinds; agents, marketing consultants, and other consultants, individuals or firms providing services or goods in connection with international business transactions.

basis in all major industrialized countries, otherwise the undesirable activity will merely move its base and there will be no level playing field of competition. Even if legislation were difficult to enforce it would have a substantial impact, argues Moody-Stuart who is a member of the UK board of TI:

> Even if prosecutions were difficult to bring, the psychological effect would be worthwhile. How often has one heard somebody say words to this effect: 'I don't much like this, but it isn't actually illegal'?

Transparency describes itself as the 'Coalition against corruption in international business transactions,' defining corruption (for the purpose of defining its own mission) as: 'The misuse of public power for private profit'. That is not intended to be a comprehensive definition of corrupt business practice, but gives a sharp focus to the body's activities. Apart from stimulating the creation of coalitions of leaders from many different walks of life to combat corruption, it also promotes an 'Islands of integrity' concept within which all leading players in a selected industry can agree simultaneously to desist from paying bribes, so creating a level playing-field. The way forward will not be easy, but bribery undermines trust; and without trust there can be no efficient economy.

Useful References

Richard T De George (1993) *Competing with Integrity in International Business*, Oxford University Press, Oxford.

George Moody-Stuart (1993) *Grand Corruption in Third World Development*, privately published, 2nd edn.

David Murray and Marek Kucia (1995) 'Business Integrity in Transitional Economies: Central & Eastern Europe', in *Business Ethics: A European Review*, April.

John T Noonan Jr (1984) *Bribes*, University of California Press, Berkeley, CA.

Part 2
Integrity in Action

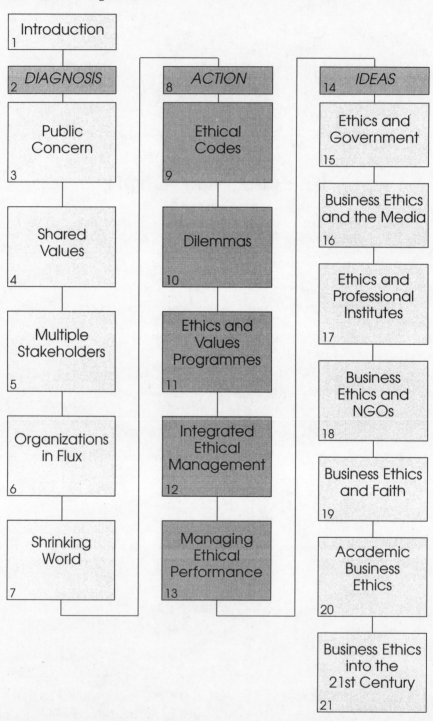

Introduction
1

DIAGNOSIS
2

Public
Concern
3

Shared
Values
4

Multiple
Stakeholders
5

Organizations
in Flux
6

Shrinking
World
7

ACTION
8

Ethical
Codes
9

Dilemmas
10

Ethics and
Values
Programmes
11

Integrated
Ethical
Management
12

Managing
Ethical
Performance
13

IDEAS
14

Ethics and
Government
15

Business Ethics
and the Media
16

Ethics and
Professional
Institutes
17

Business
Ethics and
NGOs
18

Business Ethics
and Faith
19

Academic
Business
Ethics
20

Business Ethics
into the
21st Century
21

Overview of Part 2

I f you have read through Part 1, and have worked through the
various exercises and points for challenge and reflection, you
will by now have assembled a considerable list of ethical issues
relevant to your organization. We will now look further at what
can be done about them. How can an organization systematically
approach the development of higher standards of behaviour, and
achieve a greater degree of ethical consistency in its operations?
What have other organizations around the world been doing in
recent years?

The style of this section is somewhat different from the previous
one. The main text of the chapters in Part 1 was largely descriptive,
with challenges to investigation and diagnosis contained in boxes.
In Part 2 the main text itself becomes challenging as you, the
reader, are asked to consider what you, in your organization, are
going to do about ethical development, By the time we reach Part
3 the style will change yet again, as my own views are exposed
more explicitly – about the way forward for various types of
organization, and what they should be doing to help the rest of
us.

Codes

We start with a look at how ethical codes, or codes of conduct, or
codes of practice, or corporate philosophies, or statements of
corporate business principles (they come under many names) are
being developed and used, and how you might introduce one
yourself.

A code, however, can never cover all eventualities. As has
already been explored in Chapter 4, a code which looks like a rule
book and fails to communicate the basic values or business
principles of the organization will fail to meet the needs of the
people. It may in some circumstances provide a legal defence, in
that you might be able to claim that you've tried to prevent
malpractice. I am not denying the importance of that, but in all

probability a rule book without values will eventually come to be seen by your people as little better than a corporate strait-jacket. It is important for people to understand the values on which the rules are based, so that when situations arise which are not covered by the document explicitly they can work out a viable course of action from principles. In Chapter 9 we look at some externally developed codes to which companies can choose to subscribe.

Dilemmas

Many dilemmas arise in organizational life. There may be several alternative courses of action; each has certain plus points; each has other points against; none seems to be ethically perfect; how is the choice to be made? Chapter 10 deals with this difficult area.

Integrity in Action

- How can we articulate and communicate our values and standards?

- How should we handle difficult decisions when none of the possible ways forward seems morally ideal?

- How can we get people throughout our organization to become aware of the ethical issues we all face, and equip them for the future?

- Can we prevent our many different initiatives, on quality, safety, environment, etc., indeed the whole of our business, being seen as a series of isolated activities, and bring them together as an integrated whole?

- How will we know whether we're meeting expectations, either of others or our own?

There is, of course, no simple mechanism for choice. If there were, the term 'dilemma' would lose its meaning. Many choices are always going to be hard to make, hard to communicate, and hard to sustain. While avoiding naive over-simplicity we will look at some approaches to dilemma which can at best be described as 'helps', but which I believe will move many of us a step or two forward. The decision process suggested, even if it doesn't make hard choices easy, will certainly help in explaining the choice to those affected. In the public sector, where transparency of decision making is increasingly an issue, the ability to communicate the reasoning behind complex choices can be critical to gaining public acceptance of a way forward.

Ethics Programmes

It is fine for a small number of people in an organization to study the problems of ethical behaviour, but what about the dozens, or hundreds, or even thousands of others? What about the managers who have never even thought of their business decisions as being ethical in nature? What about the people who are so busy that they look for simpler ways of working rather than adding yet more layers of complexity into their already overburdened hours? What about the people who, while sympathizing with the idea of improving standards, or of doing something to reduce the risk of serious malpractice, will nevertheless be cautious about the sustainability of any initiative? They've seen so many short-term fashionable initiatives (quality, safety, continuous improvement, environment, customer service, TQM, etc., etc.) over recent years, and can only believe that this one will go the way of the others – into forgetfulness and obscurity. How should your ethics programme be organized? This is the subject of Chapter 11 .

Integrated Ethical Management

'Initiative fatigue' is a serious problem and is now almost endemic in very many organizations. With this in mind the discussion of ethics programmes is followed immediately by Chapter 12 in which we think about a possible answer to the fatigue problem. 'Integrated ethical management' suggests an approach to viewing the various initiatives as a whole. Too often topics like quality, customer care, health and safety, and environmental responsibility are seen as isolated one from another. In fact they can be viewed as different specialist expressions of a single set of integrating values. As well as being economically important they are all, in their different ways, expressions of moral concern. We examine both the principles involved and also practical approaches in use.

Governance and Performance

What benefit does all this effort deliver? What difference is it making? How well do we comply with the requirements of external bodies, such as government regulatory agencies? How well do we perform against the criteria and improvement targets we have set ourselves? Where are the further areas for improvement? In Chapter 13, having first looked at some issues surrounding formal disciplinary action and the often thorny matter of individual performance appraisal, we take a short look at some recent developments in top level corporate governance and the increasingly popular process of ethical audit.

Into Action

The purpose of this section is to be highly practical. It will not give all the answers, nor will it provide an easy-to-follow manual of how to do it, suitable for every occasion and situation. There can be no such thing! When dealing with such matters one is treading on delicate ground. If these chapters provide people with a basic guide to mapping out a way forward it will have served a valuable purpose. If it helps them appreciate how many more questions there are to be asked than they initially expected, and that it will be uncommonly difficult and time-consuming to achieve improvement, then it will have done even better.

9

Ethical Codes

Ethical codes within business organizations are not an innovation of the 1980s and 1990s. General Robert Wood Johnson (son of the founder) of Johnson & Johnson, the worldwide health care product and services company, developed the company credo back in 1943. It continues to this day at the heart of that company's activities. J&J was not exactly a small company even in those days, but it was nothing like the size of today's organization. The credo (see the box overleaf) got in on the ground floor of the company's growth and became central to management thinking as the business expanded.

In the past 15 years an increasing proportion, especially of large organizations, has adopted this approach to corporate ethics. In the United States the development has been accelerated by the introduction of the Federal Sentencing Guidelines under which, in the event of criminal proceedings, the existence of a company code of ethics can be taken as an indication that serious efforts have been made in the organization to ensure good conduct. Elsewhere, and no doubt in many American organizations also, codes have been introduced because their leaders wish to maintain or improve standards of behaviour quite apart from the pressures of the law.

MULTIPLICITY OF CODES

How many companies have codes? That is a difficult question to answer. One sometimes hears claims to the effect that, say, 60 per cent of British companies now have codes of conduct. This seems usually to be based on averaged data from surveys such as those by Ashridge Management College in 1993, which found that 43 per cent of its respondent companies had a code, and by the Institute of Internal Auditors in 1995, which found that 70 per cent had one. In the United States the statistics are equally confusing, with different surveys producing figures which range from just over 50 per cent to well over 80 per cent. Much, of

Johnson & Johnson

Our Credo

We believe our first responsibility is to the doctors, nurses and patients, to mothers and fathers and all others who use our products and services. In meeting their needs everything we do must be of high quality. We must constantly strive to reduce our costs in order to maintain reasonable prices. Customers' orders must be serviced promptly and accurately. Our suppliers and distributors must have an opportunity to make a fair profit.

We are responsible to our employees, the men and women who work with us throughout the world. Everyone must be considered as an individual. We must respect their dignity and recognize their merit. They must have a sense of security in their jobs. Compensation must be fair and adequate, and working conditions clean, orderly and safe. We must be mindful of ways to help our employees fulfill their family responsibilities. Employees must feel free to make suggestions and complaints. There must be equal opportunity for employment, development and advancement for those qualified. We must provide competent management, and their actions must be just and ethical.

We are responsible to the communities in which we live and work and to the world community as well. We must be good citizens – support good works and charities and bear our fair share of taxes, We must encourage civic improvements and better health and education. We must maintain in good order the property we are privileged to use, protecting the environment and natural resources.

Our final responsibility is to our stockholders. Business must make a sound profit. We must experiment with new ideas. Research must be carried on, innovative programs developed and mistakes paid for. New equipment must be purchased, new facilities provided and new products launched. Reserves must be created to provide for adverse times. When we operate according to these principles, the stockholders should realize a fair return.

Printed here with permission

course, depends on the population of companies surveyed, and especially their size. It appears that the larger the firm the more likely it is to have a formal code of conduct or similar document.

Small and medium-sized organizations may well have formal written policies about individual ethical issues, such as quality, environment and human resource development, but these are rarely linked together as related entities. (On this theme there will be more to say in Chapter 12.) A survey reported in 1991 by the Dutch employers' association NCW, found that only 22 per cent of the largest 100 enterprises in the Netherlands had an ethical code as against figures ranging from 30–50 per cent in France, Germany and Britain, to 85 per cent in the USA. This difference was put down to the fact that with a few exceptions large companies in The Netherlands tend to be smaller than large companies in the other comparator countries.

AN AMAZING MULTIPLICITY OF CODES

If the number of company codes in existence is difficult to identify, once we go outside individual organizations we find an even more confusing picture. The typical professional specialist or manager may have signed half a dozen different codes in the process of joining work-related bodies.

If taken seriously, there are for most professionals far more codes to consider than the company code alone. Most of them can be, and usually are, ignored or completely forgotten. In this chapter, however, we are dealing with the development of ethical codes and it would scarcely seem ethical to ignore documents to which we and our colleagues have previously assented. The following should be taken into consideration during the code-writing process.

Just a Thought...

How many codes of conduct have you as an individual signed up to (literally or implicitly) in joining professional and industry bodies?

When did you last read any of them?

Professional Codes

Any self-respecting professional institute or association has its code of conduct. These will be examined more closely in Chapter 17. Some of them are relatively innocuous, and have not been updated for decades. Others are maintained in good order, refer to issues of the moment and reflect modern thinking.

What is more, once a manager has within his or her area of responsibility people trained in a wide variety of professions there is also a wide variety of professional codes of practice to consider. In order to avoid difficulties of this sort I have heard some specialists claim that they would refuse to work for anyone who was not professionally qualified in their own field and whom they therefore knew to have subscribed to the same principles of ethical behaviour.

Industry and Sector Codes

The next layer of codes comes from sectoral bodies. In the UK, for example, the National Health Service has its jointly published 'Code of conduct' and 'Code of accountability'. This could almost be described as a corporate code, but as the NHS now has within it a large number of trusts and authorities, each with a significant degree of independence, it also has some of the characteristics of a general industry code. Because, however, the entire NHS structure is ultimately answerable to a Secretary of State it is very firmly enforceable. Most industry codes are not like that. Many an industry association issues its members with agreed guidelines and standards covering important aspects of business behaviour in their particular sector. Generally speaking these reflect the aspirations of the leading companies in the industry, or their representatives on the drafting committees. The question has to be, even more than for the professional codes, how many people in member companies are aware of these agreed standards? They are there, and the organization has agreed to abide by them!

Single-Issue Codes

There are many single-issue codes. For example, there is the International Chamber of Commerce code on bribery and corruption; the OECD has a similar document; so also does the Berlin-based international coalition against corruption in international business, Transparency International. (TI's Standards of Conduct are shown in full in Chapter 7). During the apartheid era the South African churches developed a code of conduct for business which was extremely demanding in that political and social climate. In the United States the Coalition for Environmentally Responsible Economies (CERES) has its widely promoted 'CERES principles' (see further discussion and the text in Chapter 18). To live up to these codes, especially when the competition is thought not to, is a difficult challenge.

Codes from National and International Bodies

In addition to all the above there are codes from a wide variety of national and international business-related bodies. Probably the best known and most widely respected of the codes produced by such international groups is that from an international voluntary group of top business people, known as the Caux Principles. Several others are mentioned at various points in this book.

Implications of Multiple Codes

If one takes seriously all of these codes, to which we or our organizations or the heads of our organizations as individuals have declared some degree of allegiance, where does it lead us? Fortunately, most of them are compatible. I suggest that, in developing or revising a corporate code for your organization, one of the early steps should be to ask: 'In what professional qualifying bodies and other associations do we and our staff have membership? To what standards of behaviour have we already subscribed? How should these be taken into account in the development of our own corporate principles and practices?'

You might even like to go a step further than this. If your industry or profession has a code of conduct to which a substantial proportion of your managerial and professional staff subscribe, why not consider printing it as an appendix to your own company code? This could be especially valuable in organizations where one single professional body is strongly represented – for example, a bank, an insurance company, an accountancy practice or a legal partnership.

From a small management consultancy

Our Principles are:

- To base practical advice on the best international thinking in our fields, taking care to avoid 'quick fixes', fads and fashions.

- To work with clients who have serious intentions to improve performance, and with whom there can be partnership and mutual respect.

- To combine a business-like results-orientation with humanity, remembering that people are individuals, each with personal worth and aspirations.

- To take account of the impact of clients' origins, histories and cultures, especially when planning the pace and process of change.

- To conduct business honestly, with integrity and confidentiality.

- To provide only such services for which we are professionally competent, building a high-value image without either exaggeration or undue modesty.

- To avoid attacks on competitors, their competence and their achievements.

- To enjoy demanding work, in an atmosphere of mutual support and care.

© *Maine Consulting Services, 1991, 1996*

DEVELOPING A CODE

Ethical codes do tend to be more common in large organizations, but you do not have to be large in order to gain value from having one. My own consultancy practice, which has never employed more than four people in total, has had a 'Statement of principles' from the start. It provides a useful ongoing reminder of working principles. Also, perhaps more unusually, it is a key document in annual planning. In fact, one year most of the planned developments in consulting methodology were related to strengths and weaknesses highlighted by consideration of our principles.

There is more, however, to the development of a truly useful code than sitting down in an office for an afternoon and emerging with a ready-written document. There are several very important points to get right. You will need:

1. A clear *purpose*; you must know why you're doing this.

2. A development *process* which involves people who will be affected by the code.

3. An understanding of existing *predecessor* codes and how they function – especially external codes to which the organization and/or its individual people have subscribed.

4. A family of 'vital values' or *principles*, on which your code will be based (see Chapter 4).

5. A structure of content which is *practical* and relevant to people in the organization.

6. A two-way *promotional* process to help with communicating and implementing the code, and also (later) with obtaining feedback to help review and update it.

Clarity of Purpose

Why are you doing this? How will the code be used? What initially triggered the project? These are important questions to answer at the very beginning. There may have been a recent scandal in an organization not dissimilar to your own; you may be trying to ensure that something similar doesn't happen to you. You may feel under pressure from campaigning organizations which have targeted your industry, or even your company, and you want to make it clear to everyone that ethics matter here.

You may feel that as the organization gets bigger and more complex it is increasingly difficult to assume that everyone shares the same preconceptions about how a business should behave; you therefore want to use the code as a means of recovering some uniformity of values. You may now be operating in several countries, and believe that this is necessary to ensure consistent behaviour. You may simply feel that in an age characterized by so much greed and dishonesty you want to make a statement about the values and standards your organization still holds dear.

Whatever the reasons for producing a code, make sure that before travelling far down the development road you write them down clearly for all involved to read and ponder. Later you will need to ask whether what you have developed meets these needs.

Process of Development

It is possible to develop a code of conduct at the top level of the organization and then to impose it. Such a process, however, is unlikely to get the best results in terms of commitment. As with other aspects of management, success or failure will often be determined not by the logic or the wisdom of its content, nor by the skill with which it is communicated, but by the process used for its development.

- *Creating awareness:* first, there must be an awareness of need. Invest time in convincing people throughout the organization, at all levels, that this is not a fad, but is about meeting a real need seriously. Advance research can be an effective way of creating awareness as well as of identifying topics for inclusion in the code.

- *Identifying issues:* research, by questionnaire, interviews and group discussions, the opinions and attitudes of people from different backgrounds and with different perspectives. Discover what are the concerns of your people, and of your external stakeholders. What worries do staff take home with them about standards of behaviour in the organization they work for?

- *Involvement:* this is worth repeating. Values statements and ethical codes are too often formulated behind closed doors by groups of senior managers and specialists, and then receive the fate they deserve. Make sure that you consult widely during the development.

- *Champions:* find people from different areas and levels of the organization who will be enthusiastic and convincing advocates of the exercise; draw them into discussion about the drafting.

- *International:* remember to take account of the views of people in all the countries in which you operate, and of existing international codes. Also, consider whether you wish to establish *common values* or to impose *standard practices*. The two are not the same, and the international transferability of a 'rule book' style of code should not be taken for granted. Values may be held in common. Their detailed application may be strongly culturally determined, and may vary from country to country.

■ *Alternative styles:* you will have to consider whether you want a document which gives general principles only, or something which deals explicitly with the actual problems and dilemmas faced by people in your organization.

CHECKLIST FOR DEVELOPING AN ETHICAL CODE

Before starting the exercise:

Have you researched the views and concerns of your staff? ☐

...of managers ☐

...of your other stakeholders? ☐

Are people in the organization aware of ethics as an issue? ☐

Do you plan to develop the code in participative mode? ☐

Have you considered the role of trade unions in the project? ☐

Have you yet listed areas of current ethical concern? ☐

During and after developing the code

Is it relevant to the day-to-day lives of your people? ☐

Have you avoided creating merely a mechanistic rule book? ☐

Does it include principles to help with difficult decisions? ☐

Have you kept the number of main items to less than ten? ☐

Have you drafted guidance notes on how to use the code? ☐

Do you need supplements applying it to specific functions? ☐

Structure and Style of the Code

You will need to decide a structure for presentation of the code. It is always advisable to have something at the heart of the document which fits comfortably in quite large type on a single page to summarize the major points. From there on it is possible to expand into detail. Three widely used approaches are illustrated below. The first uses a listing of vital *corporate values* to give the primary structure. Each value statement is followed by a few concise sentences explaining what they mean in practice. (There is another important style point here. In this example, from the very impressive 'Eastman Way', the statements are phrased as if 'We are already like this.' Others prefer to phrase them as aspirations. You must choose.)

Alternative Code Structures (Examples)

Values structure

Honesty and integrity: 'We are honest with ourselves and others. Our integrity is exhibited through relationships with coworkers, customers, suppliers and neighbours. Our goal is truth in all relationships.' (Eastman Chemical Company)

Stakeholder structure

Suppliers: 'We will use our purchasing power fairly, and will: administer tendering and contracting procedures in good faith; pay promptly and as agreed.' (British Telecommunications plc)

Potential malpractice structure

Import restrictions: 'When traveling on Company business, employees must adhere to each country's laws regarding declaration and importation of money, negotiable instruments and goods. (The Quaker Oats Company)

The second uses a list of the organization's *major stakeholders* as the main structure. The third takes *areas of potential malpractice*, and structures the code around how to avoid going wrong in these critical areas. I prefer the second option, the stakeholder framework, provided that it is supported by a set of principles and that detailed conduct rules are provided separately for particularly sensitive areas of work.

I am less comfortable with the third as a primary focus, as it seems to me that it might well lead to an overemphasis on prohibition, and on ensuring defensibility in areas where there are current legal minefields, rather than on positively strengthening the moral fibre of the organization throughout all aspects of its life. Having said this, there may well be situations (probably west of the Atlantic) in which this is the more advisable form due to the highly litigious nature of society. Whatever the format, ensure that the document deals with each topic in a manner which is intelligible and appears relevant to all in the organization. Relate it to real-life problems that people face on a day-to-day basis in your company, your industry or your country.

Promotion and Training

Plan carefully how you are going to launch the code, so as to achieve both maximum exposure *and* maximum commitment. Some further aspects of this are discussed in Chapter 11 when we consider ethics programmes in broader terms.

DO CODES WORK?

Research into this leads to mixed conclusions. Chief executives who have introduced codes would generally not want to be without them. On the other hand, Donald Cressey and Charles Moore concluded in 1983 that, 'Codes have done very little to relieve the organizational pressures to be unethical.' Our next few chapters address some of the practical issues.

Useful References

Donald R Cressey and Charles A Moore (1983) 'Managerial Values and Corporate Codes of Ethics', *California Management Review*, vol 25, no 4, Summer, pp 53–77.

Series of Studies (listed below) by Simon Webley for the Institute of Business Ethics, London.

Company Philosophies and Codes of Business Ethics: A guide to their drafting and use (1988).

Business Ethics and Company Codes: Current best practice in the United Kingdom (1992).

Codes of Business Ethics: Why companies should develop them – and how (1993).

Applying Codes of Business Ethics: Report on Best Practice (1995).

10

Dilemmas

One of the areas in which corporate and professional codes rarely give any help is that of dilemmas. Some acknowledge the existence of ethical quandaries, but I have yet to see one which gives advice on how to handle them beyond, 'Talk it through with a colleague'.

One underlying cause of much management discomfort with ethical questions is this lack of commonly used and trusted thought processes for handling dilemmas. Teams made up of people from diverse professional backgrounds often have difficulty in agreeing courses of action when the choices are not easy. Much of this difficulty springs from the lack of shared processes for facing up to dilemmas.

WHAT IS A DILEMMA?

The dictionary definition of a dilemma is more than simply having to make a difficult choice. It is also about the nature of that choice

Tom's Dilemma

Tom is faced with a problem. He's on an overseas selling trip. Without a big new contract one of his two plants back home will have to close, and there is only one large order on the horizon. That is why he's here, thousands of miles from home.

Today it was made clear to him that the order is his for the taking, provided that he agrees to pay a 'commission' of a quarter of a million dollars to the brother of the country's industry minister.

The contract is big enough to stand that cost. What would you do if you were Tom?

– 'A situation that requires one to choose between two equally balanced and often equally unpleasant alternatives' or 'A predicament that seemingly defies a satisfactory solution.'

We should distinguish between a dilemma and a temptation, which is the straight choice between a 'right' and a 'wrong'. I believe, however, that it is an over-simplification to say that a dilemma is a choice between two 'rights.' More usefully we can think of it as choice between two partial rights each of which has a degree of wrong mixed in with it. This is not exactly a grey zone, but rather a speckled, heterogeneous mixture of good and bad actions and outcomes – in other words, the colour of everyday life!

Many people are uncomfortable with this idea, and prefer to think of decision making as always eliminating any 'wrong' options and then choosing only between alternative 'rights'. Some business people in Tom's position would without any consideration at all refuse to countenance the temptation to pay a bribe and would move immediately to examine the relative financial cases for closure of one of the plants. They would almost certainly consider the hardships to be imposed on the redundant workforce as unfortunate, but not as 'wrong' in the same sense as bribery. For those managers the closure decision becomes one of economic logic and not one of moral dilemma.

I am not arguing here for bribery, but for moral dilemma to be seen to include anything which goes against the vital values discussed earlier – and in most organizations there is a value statement to the effect that, 'Our people are important to us.' If an outcome of suffering for those people is seen as a 'wrong' then the initial choice about the bribe becomes a dilemma, not simply a temptation. This is so even if the wrong of bribery is still rejected – for example, on the basis that wrong acts carry 'greater wrongness' than wrong outcomes.

The first of the definitions given above refers to equally balanced alternatives. The purpose of this chapter is to help people think through dilemma situations and arrive at a point where the options no longer seem equally balanced, where although there may still be no ideal way forward a defensible choice can be made.

MAKING HARD CHOICES

Complex decisions and policy making always involve trade-offs. Where we have several options and yet none seems ideal we need to scan for even further options; creativity is needed; lateral-thought becomes essential to generate yet more possible ways forward. Different principles or values pull us in opposite directions. We must decide not only how to understand the facts of the situation but also how to weight our various principles, our sense of the rights and wrongs of the alternative courses of action (deontology), and of the desirability of different outcomes (teleology).

The situation is not helped (from the typical manager's point of view) by the fact that we live in an increasingly transparent society. Decisions which 20 or 30 years ago would have been taken behind closed doors are now taken in various types of open forum. Even when that is not the case the newspapers, radio or television may well decide to explore the issues in the open, not necessarily with the benefit of comprehensive information. Hard managerial choices often have to be explained openly, to a degree unheard of in the past – and not only in public sector organizations but increasingly also in private sector business.

It is important for decisions to be defensible even when they are not ideal. Also, the public must be educated in the realities of decision making under conditions of uncertainty, ambiguity and dilemma, but this will not be possible until more sensitive managerial decisions are made by processes more rigorous than are commonplace today.

A DECISION PROCESS

From the start it must be emphasized that there can be no rigid, structured method that will automatically give us 'right' answers. We will at many stages be confronted with the need to make judgements. Not everything is quantifiable. Not everything is predictable. We should, however, be able to structure and record our judgements so that our eventual decisions are at the very least explicable, even if not to everyone justifiable.

The following outline is similar in principle to that described by Kent Hodgson in his excellent book, *A Rock and a Hard Place*, although not identical and it was initially developed quite independently. While not following him in every respect I recommend Hodgson's book as very thought-provoking.

Resolving Dilemmas

A Process to Help Reasoning

Situation

- What are the 'facts' of the situation? What are the 'root causes'? What are the risks and opportunities?

- Who are/will be involved/affected, ie, who are the stakeholders? Have you identified them all? *Are you sure?*

- Do any of the stakeholders perceive the 'facts' differently?

Alternatives

- What are the options? Are these *all* the options? Have you applied creative thinking methods? Are there *no* others?

- What will be the consequences of each option for each stakeholder? Who is/are likely to be for and against each of the options, and on what grounds?

Analysis

- Which of your 'vital values' or other criteria derived from them are relevant to this decision? Create a list of decision criteria, including financial, technical and other requirements.

- Are you clear in your mind as to where/whether you are judging on the basis of the rightness of acts (deontology) and/or the desirability of outcomes (teleology)?

- How does each option rate against your list of criteria?

- Can you make a clear choice? Do any of the options definitely eliminate themselves? Can you select a short-list?

■ Think laterally. Are you sure there are no further alternatives?

■ Which of your decision criteria (including the relevant basic values) are more important than the others? Rank the list.

Choice

■ Choose, taking greater account of the more important criteria.

■ Your chosen option will have some 'downside' aspects, or you didn't really have a dilemma in the first place. How can you minimize these? Are there lessons from discarded options?

■ What are the communication issues flowing from the decision? How are you going to face each of the predictable objections?

The Logical Process

The first stages in the 'Resolving dilemmas' box are to establish what are the facts and the options. Then criteria are needed in order to make rational decisions, and in the world of dilemma these criteria will to a substantial degree be moral in nature. Traditional business decision criteria relating to technology, finance and logistics will still have their very important places. They are not superseded, but neither must they be allowed to crowd out ethical considerations.

It will be very noticeable to some that I am not pressing here for the use of a numerical decision matrix, allocating numerical ratings to each of the options against each of the criteria, and possibly also with numerical weights to the criteria. I do not deny the value of such methods. I have myself used them often. However, when dealing with 'value judgements about values' it is too easy to be deceived by the apparent precision of the numbers. I recommend using such methods with care. It must never be forgotten that the eventual numbers are no more than a convenient quantitative shorthand to summarize a set of complex qualitative judgements.

The Human Process

The human process is not considered in the box, and yet this can be vital. The design of decision-making groups in difficult situations can be the determinant of eventual success – that is, of achieving anything like a consensus. This is not the place for extensive treatment of this aspect of our subject. I recommend reading Graham Wilson's book in this series, *Problem Solving and Decision Making*. It provides a useful introduction to the human aspects.

Many of us, of course, *instinctively* go through a similar process when we make hard choices, and you might ask what all the fuss is about. The sequence is not complicated after all.

Decisions in organizations are not always made by thinking matters through comprehensively – and indeed not all decisions can be dealt with in such a time-consuming manner. It is not always easy to detect in advance which dilemma choices will be the ones to cause the problems afterwards. Managers are not especially gifted with foreknowledge, and this is all the more reason why such processes as this should be practised (and adapted by each organization to suit its own circumstances) so that eventually much of the logic becomes almost natural behaviour. When we do articulate a difficult decision systematically in this way we will feel considerably more secure, and be equipped better to explain and defend our actions.

ALTERNATIVE APPROACHES

Much more could be written on this topic. There are no simple and totally satisfying solutions to genuine dilemmas. Considerably more thought needs to be given to this by managers, specialist professionals and moral philosophers, so that professional development programmes can better prepare people for the real-life quandaries they will inevitably face. Two interesting approaches are outlined by Jack Mahoney (The principle of double effect) and Rushworth Kidder (including a model of four 'Dilemma paradigms') in short articles quoted in the references below.

Useful References

Kent Hodgson (1992) *A Rock and A Hard Place: How to make ethical business decisions when the choices are tough*, American Management Association, New York.

Rushworth Kidder (1996) 'Reaching for what's right', *Organisations & People*, vol 3 no 2, May.

Jack Mahoney (1996) 'Balancing good and bad effects', *Organisations & People*, vol 3 no 2, May.

Graham Wilson (1993) *Problem Solving and Decision Making*, The Fast-Track MBA Series, Kogan Page, London.

11

Ethics and Values Programmes

This chapter is a close follow-on from Chapter 9, in which we looked at the development of an organizational code of conduct. Not every ethics programme must of necessity have a code at its heart, but the majority almost certainly will do so. Here it is assumed that a code, or at the very least a statement of corporate values, has been developed and that the next step is to decide how to ensure that this makes a real difference, rather than simply being seen as yet one more action point on the board's list, ticked off as 'done' and then forgotten.

We will start by revisiting some key points about the development of the code. First, then, some questions:

- Did you create an awareness of the need, and of the exercise, throughout the organization early in the process of developing the code?

- Did you involve as many people as possible in its development?

- Did you research what are the concerns about ethical issues, not only of people in your organization but also of your major external stakeholders?

- Did you articulate a set of 'vital values' (you may choose to describe them in different words, but they're no less vital) as a foundation upon which to build the code?

- Did you ensure that the values were phrased and explained so as not to be vague, but to make it possible to assess after a period of time whether they are actually being implemented in practice?

- Did you identify 'champions' throughout the organization to act as enthusiastic advocates of the process?

- Did you make a considered decision about the style of your document, including whether to structure it around values, stakeholder relationships or potential areas of malpractice?

- Did you avoid making the code too much like a rule book?

- Did you decide whether it would need supplements to deal in greater detail with specific problem areas?

- Did you relate it to other documents, such as an existing mission statement, and to policy statements such as those on quality, environment, and health and safety? (See Chapter 12 for more on this.)

This chapter is written in the form of concise paragraphs to highlight the key points in an ethics and values programme. Each brief point could well take up several pages in its own right, but the aim here is to be action-oriented rather than to enter upon theoretical debate. Many of the points raised are not unique to this particular field of endeavour. They are matters which have to be considered in any kind of change programme, and in any participative activity. An ethics and values programme, although it does certainly have some features of its own, also shares many features with other types of people-oriented project.

COMMUNICATION

Now that you have determined the content and the wording, how (and to whom) will you communicate your code or values statement?

You will almost certainly wish to publish it in some form to all employees. Are there other groups who ought to be informed about the principles on which you are going to operate in the future? If you are a public body, such as a local authority or a health authority or trust, you may wish to publish it to the local population, or to the 'customers' of each type of service – in which case you will probably need to work out in further detail just what it will mean for them in practical reality, so that you can make the document relevant. You should avoid publishing documents phrased in managerial jargon and current fad-language. Indeed, you should avoid using such unattractive, and frequently meaningless, language internally; it merely confirms staff in their view that managers don't understand the words they use.

If you already have a staff newsletter you might use this to get the message across. An existing system of briefing groups and management meetings can also be valuable. Both together will be even better. If you have already used your briefing groups or quality circles to consult about the content you will already be halfway there, but do ensure that such groups are working before relying on them.

You will probably publish your values as a separate document, but try to ensure that it isn't seen as 'Just another piece of waste paper'! Make it attractive. Use forceful design to ensure that the key messages are communicated to the kind of people that you have in your business. For example, a young, artistic organization will have different design needs from a traditional engineering company. Why not consider putting a hypertext version on your computer network, or distributing it to PC users as a Windows Help file?

In a widely distributed organization the external media could also be used, and this would have the advantage of getting the message across to external stakeholders also. Take care, however, that you pay adequate attention to thinking through the most likely public responses, so that you have well-formulated answers available when the predictable criticisms come back at you.

Do you want people to sign their 'allegiance'? Some organizations require their managers and staff periodically to sign a reaffirmation of commitment to their code of conduct. This is certainly one possible way of keeping it to the front of people's minds, but remember that it can backfire. You don't want your staff to respond with accusations that you're implying their past behaviour to have been less than commendable. The current organizational climate will determine whether (or when) this is appropriate.

PLANNING THE LAUNCH

Take care. You will be creating impressions that will last a long time. If your values emphasize economy, for example, ask what message will be communicated by a lavishly illustrated and expensive booklet. At the same time, ensure that the launch causes 'ripples' throughout the organization. It should not be 'Just another policy paper'.

It has been stressed many times already that the code should not be developed at the top only. Having said this, top-level leadership is important. If the chief executive is not fully behind this, and does not intend to apply the values and the code to the work of the top team, then you should ask whether it is worth wasting good time and money on what will probably be a pointless exercise.

A serious attempt to understand people's concerns and to draw a representative cross-section of managers and staff into the formulation process should already have reduced the risk of widespread cynical response. There will always be some, however. The important point is to demonstrate that you really are sincere, and are determined to make a permanent impact. Start living the values well before they're published, and don't ever claim to live up to all of them 100 per cent. Admit that you do sometimes get things wrong. However naive this may seem, honesty is ultimately respected.

We live in an age of managerial miracle cures and passing fashions. Make it clear that you are aware of this, and even admit that this might have been characteristic of some of your organization's past initiatives. Make the point that the lesson has been learned, that this is 'for real' and that you are aware that to reach anywhere near the ideals will take a long haul.

Like other things the code will lose its lustre after a period of time and will require a re-launch. Ensuring that it is in regular use should delay this requirement, especially if an annual review of progress is carried out and even more so if the code is seen to be an important strand in strategic and operational planning processes.

TRAINING

Promotional campaigns and glossy launches don't change behaviour in an organization to any significant degree. They have to be followed up by continual reinforcement of the message. It must be seen that the organization is serious about its espoused values. One of the most powerful ways of achieving this is to ensure that these new principles of conduct are incorporated in every aspect of training.

All activities of the organization should relate naturally to what it claims to value. If you are not prepared for this it will rapidly become clear that the pretence of valuing the publicized values is little more than a public relations exercise.

New managers and staff should be made familiar in their induction training with the code and/or values statement, and also with how people are expected to use it. In fact, at least for senior positions and for jobs involving external contact, a discussion of values and their significance should have taken place at the recruitment stage. Training on matters such as performance

Before communicating the values:

1. Have you thought carefully about who are your audiences? ☐

2. Will you communicate the values to external stakeholders? ☐

3. Will you be explaining the values to 'customers'/'clients'? ☐

4. Has the process been communicated clearly to staff? ☐

5. Is further communication needed by staff? ☐

6. Is any consultation/negotiation with unions still required? ☐

7. Will you be asking staff to sign allegiance to the values/code? ☐

Launching the values, and training

8. Have you taken precautions against widespread cynicism? ☐

9. Have you distinguished this from a 'latest passing craze'? ☐

10. Is the top team *totally* behind this? If not...? ☐

11. Are plans in place to build values into staff training? ☐

12. Are plans in place to include values in director training? ☐

13. Are self-managed learning materials available? ☐

planning and review, management style and customer care should be based on values. In public organizations, in the training of both appointed and elected officials it is important that one or more leading figures in the organization should explain how the code and its underlying values apply to their work and how they are to be used in practice.

If you have a learning centre or library for employees, especially if it is being developed as a resource for self-managed learning and continuing professional development, you should incorporate materials (books, etc.) on the ethics and values of public service and/or business life. For an excellent example of how to use modern technology in ethics training, call the MIT Ethics Center for Engineering and Science on the Internet World Wide Web and (among others) look at the Lockheed Martin cases at http://web.mit.edu/ethics/www/martin.html

MAKING THE VALUES REAL

One of the chief problems with many codes and statements of 'values' is that they do not seem relevant to the day-to-day lives of people in their jobs. This is a real problem, because it is virtually impossible in any large or complex organization to write a document which will cover every situation and dilemma.

Two main alternative courses of action are open: (i) to use the general values statement of the overall organization as a basis from which to develop a series of more localized codes; and (ii) to provide training in how to apply the general code to specific circumstances, so that people can localize it for themselves. I do not recommend one above the other. Both approaches are workable. Both take a great deal of work.

Ethics training should recognize that there are varying needs throughout the organization. Cascading organizational values or a code of conduct into specialist functions (such as personnel, finance and information technology) will mean recognizing the different emphases within these areas of work. The personnel and finance functions are easily recognized as areas in which ethical issues come to the fore, although in each it is very easy to assume that provided one's actions are not actually illegal then they must be ethical. In the IT function, as in other types of technical work, some may feel that the work is ethically neutral, but issues such as access, confidentiality and the enshrining of unfair, even if long-standing, practices into computerized systems are now providing an ethical challenge to many thoughtful professionals.

As has repeatedly been emphasized since we looked at stake-holders in depth in Chapter 5, relationships with a wide variety of people and bodies (internal and external) on whom the organization has an impact require careful thought. A customer charter will be all the better for showing how its provisions flow from the organization's values. If a charter already exists a good training exercise would be to critique it in groups, in the light both of the values and of people's knowledge of how customers are treated in actual day-to-day working life.

The kinds of decisions made at different levels in an organization vary considerably. In many public bodies there is the additional dimension of an elected member or officer structure. Each gives rise to its own particular ethical dilemmas. In communication and training these should be given special attention. For many elected officials and representatives there is the additional complicating factor of political belief. In many instances ethics and politics will intertwine. Distinctions should be made between differences between people in their political objectives and differences between them in the practical policies which they prefer as means of achieving those objectives. Ethical debate may be triggered at either level.

Many of the ethical dilemmas of top management will be about overall direction and strategic choices, with long timescales, considerable uncertainty and inevitably inadequate information. In middle management the dilemmas are often related to being 'sandwiched' between the strategic and the operational, about pressures to perform against targets with which one may not agree, and implementing hard decisions taken by others.

Then there are the staff at the 'sharp end'. Ask junior staff and others who deal directly with your major stakeholders, 'What are the moral issues you face on a day-to-day basis?' You may get some uncomfortable answers which will test your commitment to the principle of managing by values.

Don't forget the ethical difficulties which come with different managerial situations. There is no point in launching a values code which stresses being nice to people if three weeks later you're going to be making a hundred staff redundant. Of course, making people redundant is not necessarily unethical (indeed, sometimes it can be the only ethical, however uncomfortable, thing to do). Make clear from the start that real life is not always simple and that in situations where no solution is perfect for everyone difficult trade-offs have to be made. Values will very often be in tension with one another. As discussed in Chapter 10, training will be needed to help people in the resolution of dilemmas.

Making it Real – Ethics in Decision Making

In many organizations introducing an ethical question into a business decision would be considered a most strange and unusual thing to do. At the other end of the spectrum (see Figure 11.1) some organizations (a minority) have ethical criteria built into formal decision processes as a natural and expected component alongside other factors such as technical and financial. You might find it helpful to consider where on the spectrum your own organization, or its various parts, currently resides.

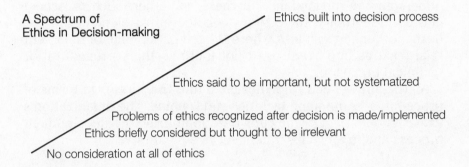

A Spectrum of
Ethics in Decision-making

Ethics built into decision process

Ethics said to be important, but not systematized

Problems of ethics recognized after decision is made/implemented
Ethics briefly considered but thought to be irrelevant
No consideration at all of ethics

Figure 11.1 *Ethics in organizational decision-making – a spectrum*

Making it Real – The Design of Services

The application of ethical thinking to product and service design is a relatively new concept in most organizations. It is discussed here, using the design of personal human services as an example to illustrate the use of values and ethics in daily managerial and professional work.

Especially in the field of human services, person-to-person care, the close relationship between quality and customer-focus on the one hand, and ethics and values on the other is increasingly coming to be appreciated. The way we treat people is an ethical issue.

Many services have never been designed systematically; they have simply happened. This, however, is changing. The need to design a service as rigorously as one would design a manufactured product is increasingly recognized. Each service should be specified at three levels: (i) what the client/customer will receive/ experience; (ii) what the provider needs to do in order to deliver this to the client; (iii) the means by which the service organization will know that the work has been done effectively. In some services there is an additional dimension, that of monitoring not only the service delivery (or 'Output') but also its long-term effect or 'Outcome'.

Concentrating for the moment on the delivery of the service, a values-driven approach to specification will consider issues of humanity, whether in a transient encounter or a long-term relationship. Timeliness, responsiveness and flexibility, courtesy and friendliness, availability and access, sympathy and support, understanding and guidance; all these, and others such as respect and confidentiality, have to be considered as elements in the design of human services where the felt experience of the client is at least as important as, if not more so than, procedural or technical precision.

All the above need to be designed into the service in terms of procedures, equipment, facilities and training. The organization's values should be a prime consideration during the development process and in any subsequent service reviews.

DAY-TO-DAY CONDUCT

Values are not only about the 'big' issues in an organization. They are also about how we work together from day to day.

Your code or values statement may or may not itself incorporate specific references to such topics as sexual harassment, non-discrimination and equal opportunities. It should, however, be framed so that it is easy to derive from it policies on these and other aspects of conduct at work. It should also provide a basis on which to build training on such problem themes in a way which is convincing even to people who might otherwise consider them to be matters only for campaigning special interest groups.

It is not my intention to suggest here that there is only one desirable management style. The choice of an effective style must to some extent be influenced by the circumstance faced. Having said this, there are undesirable styles of managerial behaviour (such as arrogance, condescension and bullying). These are ethical issues.

Some organizations are highly competitive internally; this may not be entirely inappropriate, but it will carry with it risks of dishonesty, back-stabbing and character assassination. Training in the organization's values, if suitably formulated, should help to avoid this – or you may wish the code explicitly to encourage team working in sharp contrast to individualist competition.

Ask yourself whether 'The way that management is done' fits with your declared values. Is too much done behind closed doors?

Are the people affected by decisions whenever possible involved in them, or at least kept appropriately informed? How do you balance participation and speed? What do your values have to say to these issues?

Is the performance of individuals thought of solely in terms of whether they've reached certain numerical targets? Or are you concerned also about *how* they've achieved their results? Does your financial reward system confirm or contradict your alleged values? We will return to this theme in Chapter 13.

MONITORING PROGRESS

You will wish to check whether or not you are making progress. In Chapter 13 we will look briefly at ethical audit as a process, but here are a few other practical thoughts on the subject.

You might establish a review group, representative of people from throughout the organization, to discuss annually what has been learned from the past year's practical use of the code, and to suggest improvements to either its content or its presentation.

This group might be responsible for agreeing a (small) number of performance measures which can be monitored. After all, you will want to know and to be able to demonstrate whether the programme is having its desired impact. This will be unique to your organization. Only you know what are the problems currently faced. You might, however, include such objectives as complaint reduction, improved organizational 'climate', or selected aspects of external reputation. Many of these may already be measured, or assessed in some non-quantitative way, in which case you will simply be assembling them in a different format as indicators of ethical development. Do not fall into the trap of attempting to measure everything, or of feeling that it is always necessary to measure new things.

Monitoring should be seen as a key element in corporate governance. Decide who, at the top, are going to form the oversight group, then provide them with necessary information. Complaints analyses, feedback from briefing groups, questionnaires to a sample of managers and staff, 'customer feedback' questionnaires, and reports from facilitated discussions with groups of staff and/or clients are just some of the possibilities.

A further possibility is to combine with a number of similar or related organizations (maybe competitors – depending on the commercial and legal situation). Possibly you might use the services of an independent body to develop a benchmark scoring system for a series of factors considered by all involved to be important, and to run periodic comparative checks. Recommendations of best practice could emerge from such studies.

'Whistleblowing'

There can be situations in which managers and staff feel particularly strongly about what they see as ethical issues, but have no 'safe' route by which to get their concern heard. You should consider the possibility of establishing a confidential 'whistleblowing' procedure.

Evaluation processes

1. Have you appointed a *top level* monitoring group? ☐
2. Do you have systems for providing it with necessary data? ☐
3. Do you have a 'conscience' or 'whistleblowing' process? ☐
4. Will you be 'benchmarking' against other organizations? ☐
5. Do you intend to use a 'values monitor' questionnaire? ☐
6. Is performance against values on management agendas? ☐
7. Is performance against values on board agendas? ☐

Practical application

8. Are values built into the strategic planning process? ☐
9. Are values used as a common basis for specialist policies? ☐
10. Are values used in making major business decisions? ☐
11. Are products/services designed by reference to the values? ☐
12. Are management style/processes consistent with the values? ☐
13. Do staff view values as important in all aspects of work? ☐

CAN THIS BE REAL?

It might be argued, and with some justification, that much in the preceding pages is somewhat idealistic. In the real world these things take time, and not all of these important components of a values programme can be done at once. We must therefore come down to earth.

Figure 11.2 illustrates, in simplified form, the sequence of planning and implementation processes in a service organization. An unusual feature is the inclusion of 'values' at its heart. There is no start or finish to the process. The intervention must be made at some opportune moment as the cycle is spinning round. Life will not stand still for the benefit of this initiative.

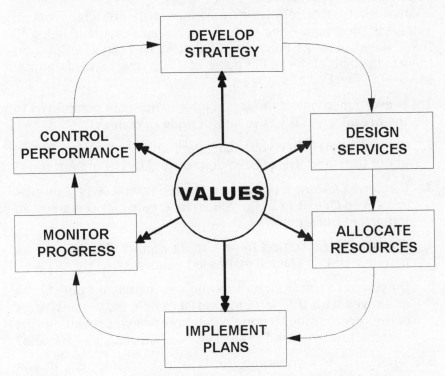

Figure 11.2   *Values-focused planning and operation cycle*

It may be appropriate to develop the values in the run-up to a new round of annual planning, building them into the strategy formulation process. Alternatively you might start at the implementation stage of the cycle. It is not essential to promote the values heavily in all parts or aspects of the organization simultaneously, or in any particular order.

Starting from where you are

People often would like to start a journey from some place other than where they are. For the introduction of a code of conduct or organizational values, just like other journeys, you don't have the option. You are where you are! The important thing is to understand the current condition of the organization, and the likely reaction to the launch of the initiative. This will determine just how, precisely when, and in what sequence you decide to launch and to initiate application to different functions, departments, processes and policy areas.

Answers to the following questions will not give you an automatic programme design, but your responses should help you think ahead of some common difficulties and pitfalls. Consider them in the light of the earlier pages of this chapter and of Chapter 9.

1. Is every member of the top management team committed to the organizational values and/or code of conduct?

2. Do you know what your managers and staff currently feel about the standards of behaviour of, and in, the organization?

3. If you don't know already, how do you intend to find out the answer to Question 2? Do you, in fact, consider this to be an important question?

4. Does the organization have a track record of acting on its people's and its clients' expressed concerns?

5. Do you have a tradition of developing significant policies or initiatives with the participation of people from many parts of the organization? If you do not, how will you set about this exercise in such a mode as will give a good chance of success?

6. What else is happening, or is about to happen, in the organization? Do you intend to ensure that everything in these initiatives is consistent with your newly articulated principles?

7. Why are you doing this?

Finally, a reminder: 'Values are what you value above all else.'

12

Integrated Ethical Management

Many companies today are suffering from what is commonly becoming known as 'initiative fatigue'. A wide variety of corporate initiatives succeed one another with amazing rapidity, covering everything from quality to the environment to delegation and empowerment. Top executives, while publicly behind all of these good things are privately heard to groan, 'Surely, not another subject that "can only be handled from the top"! When will it all end?' Specialist managers and their multiplicity of external consultants line up to appeal for the special attention of the top people. 'If we're going to make a real difference in this organization', they proclaim, 'this programme simply must be launched by the chief executive. He must stay behind it and demonstrate his commitment in real, practical ways consistently over time.' The Chief Executive rapidly tires of his (or her) irreplaceability.

By the time these programmes reach the middle and junior management levels, and even more so by the time they arrive with the bulk of the staff, the groans are heard even louder. 'Not another flash in the pan!' 'Where do they dream up these schemes? It will only last three months, mark my word.' 'I wish I had a pound for every new programme I've seen here over the past 20 years.' 'It will go the same way as TQM. Who ever hears of that around here these days?'

These Good Things Must Not Go Wrong!

The difficulty is that these many initiatives are probably all dealing with important issues for the organization. Companies cannot afford to fail with programmes aimed at improving quality and efficiency, or serving their customers better, or reducing environmental impact. Some way must be found of ensuring that such initiatives get the attention they need at all levels – but without the fatigue. In this chapter I make some suggestions, based on pulling together many of the strands which we have covered in

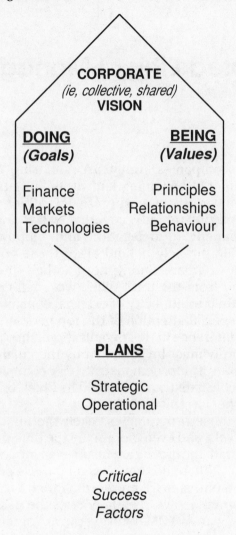

Figure 12.1   *Doing and being*

previous chapters. They are probably not totally novel, but they certainly are rarely practised.

First, though, why do high profile corporate initiatives go wrong? Here are some common reasons:

- They're hyped up to promise more than is realistic.

- They're presented as add-ons to management instead of being at the heart of it.

- Each programme is sponsored by a different specialist group, each believing theirs is the most important.

- There are few if any common threads between them all.

- Many of them (such as quality assurance, environment, continuous improvement, and training) often involve external auditors – and different auditors, often with little commonality between their approaches, leading to high costs in staff and management time.

THE 'VISION THING'

Back in 1989 I carried out an investigation to discover what the relatively few organizations which then had started to talk about 'corporate vision' actually meant by it. First I found that some talked about 'vision' while others talked about 'mission'. There was little difference in what they meant by the two words. Second, and I mentioned this in Chapter 1, I discovered that they fell largely into two groups: those which emphasized their achievement goals in terms of financial performance, markets and technology, and those which stressed the kind of organization they wished to have in terms of principles and values. Very few brought the two together.

Figure 12.1 shows the way in which at that stage I began to see the strands coming together – a 'vision' of the organization's future, in terms of both doing and being, flowing into strategic and operational plans, and ensuring that the few critical determinants of success (that is, success as defined by *both* strands of the vision) are addressed within the plans.

As time has passed I still have found relatively few organizations which are comfortable with this kind of approach. Why? Possibly because it does not incorporate a process for bringing it down to earth. And yet, much of the necessary machinery is already in place in many companies. We need an integrating model to show that what are currently viewed as separate entities are actually part of a single whole. Before going to that, however, we must ask an important question.

WHAT ARE THE ETHICAL FUNCTIONS OF A BUSINESS?

In one sense, as we saw in Chapter 5, all functions have ethical dimensions to them. Each has stakeholders, and therefore

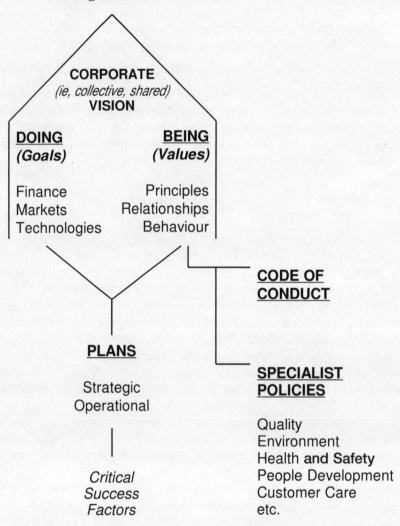

Figure 12.2   *Integrated ethical management – a map*

relationships. In some, however, matters of ethics come more to the fore, as their very existence flows from principle. I suggest that, whether carried out by specialist departments or with responsibilities for them distributed throughout the organization to a multiplicity of individual managers, the following functions have such major ethical components that they are worthy of the name: *'primary ethical functions'*.

Personnel – Quality and Customer Care
Security – Health and Safety – Environmental Impact

There may be others that you would wish to add, which are especially important to your particular kind of organization. Ponder for a few minutes what these might be, and on what basis you are identifying them,

PULLING IT ALL TOGETHER

One approach currently being promoted in some circles for bringing many of these themes together is the international standardization of 'management systems' (in reality an exaggeration as they deal with technical administration, not with management in its totality). The ISO 9000 series of standards for quality assurance has made a major contribution to many industries over recent years by imposing order where too many organizations had administrative chaos. By identifying 20 areas in which many companies had weak technical and production administrative systems, these standards, and in the UK their predecessor BS 5750, have delivered considerable improvements in performance – although when imposed inappropriately they have also caused some problems, as with any allegedly universal standard. The use of external, third party, systems audit in conjunction with these standards has also had a largely beneficial impact (although again, not without some problems).

The temptation, therefore, is to argue (as is currently being done enthusiastically in many international standardization committees) for an integrated standard to cover all such administrative systems and then an integrated process of third-party audit. I cannot imagine anything less likely than such a mechanistic approach to win the hearts and minds of managers and staff throughout British industry, and I suspect the same will be true in other countries also.

The Chemical Industries Association has its 'Responsible care' programme (initially developed in Canada) which brings together much of what we are discussing here. There appears to be, however, an increasing tendency to link this to enforceable audit processes, which some fear will result in its being seen eventually as bureaucratic red tape. I suspect that these doubters may be proved right.

Figure 12.2 illustrates my proposal which does not, by leaving them out of the picture, deny the usefulness of standards and audit but does not put the emphasis there. The heart of the matter is human motivation. The primary core of the human integrating process is the application of 'vision and values', and these must permeate all of the organization's processes of strategy formation, business planning and operational control. Otherwise these will continue to be fragmented, mechanistic and uninspiring.

I make four practical suggestions in closing this chapter:

- Place the emphasis on the organization's *vital values and code*, and present all other specialist policies as practical implementations of these.

- Ensure that there are many *effective cross-linkages* between
  (a)   your values and code, with their implementing policies,
  (b)   your strategic and operational planning,
  (c)   building your corporate culture, and
  (d)   identifying and managing your critical success factors.

- Train managers and staff in the tools and thought processes of *improvement* in a way which makes them relevant to all of the ethical functions, not only to one – such as quality or environment. This training will, if appropriately designed, constitute a further integrating force.

- Use *audit* carefully and *only* as a tool to help improvement. This may not always be easy, given external demands from powerful customers, but do your utmost to avoid introducing it as an imposed, blame-focused policing system.

Managing Ethical Performance

A s has been mentioned repeatedly in earlier chapters, moral issues in business and other organizations need to be considered at many levels. In this chapter we will look at some issues of ethical performance at the levels of:

- the individual;
- the economic system (national and global);
- the organization (and its component functions).

INDIVIDUAL ETHICAL ISSUES

Much consideration is given within personnel and human resource departments as to how to deal with infractions of company rules such as poor timekeeping, or bringing alcohol onto the premises, or failing to wear protective clothing, or petty pilfering or even (in some organizations with an extreme sense of correctness) accepting the gift of a cup of coffee from a potential supplier.

Applying the Rule Book

There are two considerations here. First, there is the question of whether the rule or standard is a sensible one, whether there are indeed ethical challenges to be brought against the rule book itself. Every organization should have some process by which this kind of challenge can be raised, preferably when there is no emotionally charged case in progress. A continuous improvement suggestion process might be an appropriate route for relatively minor matters. Remember that *rules are not principles*. After being in place for many years they come to feel like that, but they are not. They are intended to help give practical expression to the ethical principles and core values of the organization. Periodically they need to be reviewed to check whether they really do so.

Second, there are questions about how to deal with specific instances as they arise. It is not too long since most organizations allowed so much flexibility in their disciplinary proceedings that the whim of the manager or supervisor was the law. Too many organizations are still like this, although probably most people reading this book will work in environments where there are reasonably comprehensive and well-defined processes and penalties. Especially as organizations grow larger they need to enshrine moral principle into rules of practice, and to have standard arrangements for dealing with matters when they go wrong. This in itself, however, gives rise to difficulties; the rule book too easily becomes inflexible and inhumane. What was intended to be an instrument of morality becomes an unethical straitjacket. Here, then are some suggestions for you to consider en route to humanizing the rule book.

- *Consistency* – fairness is an important issue; there may even be legal implications to treating different cases differently, and one should always divert from the normal procedures with caution. That is one reason why organizations have rules and rule books. However, disciplinary situations are rarely identical. They deal with all the rich diversity of human life and frailty, and therefore inevitably lead to dilemmas. By all means have an aspiration to consistency, but don't over-simplify this. There are three further Cs to consider.

- *Causes* – remember to investigate what lies behind the problem; often there are hidden causes which may be treatable with help from the organization, and may even have been caused by something within your organization's ways of working, which you should ensure is attended to.

- *Consequences* – remember that disciplinary action frequently has unexpected consequences. Try to consider what these might be. Broadly based moral decision making takes account of the consequences of actions as well as the actions themselves. There are often many stakeholders. Not only does the organization as a whole have its multiple stakeholders; so also does every action you take. Disciplinary action inevitably affects a multiplicity of people. Whilst the tendency in many instances is simply to do 'what is right' according to the rule book, and to take action against the offender, slow down first to ask who else will be affected, and how you will deal with this.

■ *Care* – without becoming sloppy or allowing discipline to fall into ruin, consider the full range of the organization's values, including those of care for people and their development. Is there some way in which the individual can be helped to recover, either following or in place of hard disciplinary action?

Appraising Individual Performance

Few topics are as likely to lead to a heated discussion among human resource professionals as the rights and wrongs of various approaches to individual performance appraisal. This is a large subject which cannot be addressed comprehensively here. The box below contains just some of the questions frequently raised. From here on I will assume that some form of performance appraisal is in place, and will focus on two questions which I believe are of profound ethical significance, and are at the root of the failure of many such schemes and their related payment systems. The first concerns the individualism built into most such systems, while the second relates to the narrow basis on which people are too often appraised. I will express my concerns in two questions:

Performance Appraisal
Some of the moral questions to ask of a system

Who sets targets?

Who appraises?

Does it reflect teamwork?

How consistent is it?

Who decides rewards, and how?

■ In your appraisal system do the 'objectives' or 'targets' or 'criteria' laid down for an individual (however derived, whether consultatively or imposed) truly reflect the performance of that one person?

■ Does your performance review system take into account not only *what* has been achieved, but also *how* it has been achieved?

If the answer to either or both of these questions is, 'No', and your organization has a statement of values including such ideals as fairness and truth and care for people, then you should seriously consider whether or not your performance management system is unethical (by your own declared standards).

Increasingly, it is impossible to attribute the successful performance of a task or completion of a project to a single individual. People in organizations are interdependent, and yet year after year individuals are assessed as if they worked in isolation from all interaction with others. In setting the next year's targets rarely are the questions asked: 'On whom will I depend in order to achieve these?' and 'Who will depend on me to achieve their objectives?' Throughout most of the world of performance appraisal the fallacy of almost universal 'primary' individualistic accountability is perpetuated, while the 'sharing' of accountability is viewed by many almost as a heresy. This is not how most organizations actually work. It leads to hundreds of thousands of people annually being appraised against a fiction.

The second of the two ethical points concerns the *content* of the performance review. How often is it the case that a person achieves his or her targets, even exceeds them handsomely, but does so only by treading on others? Rarely is credit for anything shared by such an individual. Indeed, if someone else's reputation has to be blackened in order to boost his or her own position, then so be it. If a longstanding professional relationship between a colleague and a high-spending customer has to be undermined in order to help him or her take over the account, that's seen as just part of the game.

Is it? Not according to the values of help and cooperation between colleagues declared so glowingly in the recruitment brochures! If a company truly believes in its statements of principle it will apply them to *all* of its processes, including the assurance of justice in the review and reward of individual performance.

PERFORMANCE OF AN ECONOMIC SYSTEM

We will look quickly at the level of the economic system before refocusing on the ethical performance of the organization itself. The question must be raised, even if only briefly. 'What criteria should be used in assessing the performance of an economy?' Should they be solely numerical, financial? Or should they also take account of less quantifiable factors such as the general health of society? These are not, as some would argue, questions of little or no relevance to senior managers. Organizations operate within economic, political and social environments, and are influenced by those environments – but also they in turn help to shape them.

Rather than debate questions about national or global economies, which even for most senior managers are rather remote, here are three challenges to consider concerning the potential wider impact of *your* organization. It will in some degree influence developments in society – either local, national or global according to the scale and significance of its operations.

- Does the way we run this business exemplify to society an attitude of enlightened self-interest, concerned also for the well-being of others, or a climate of self-centred greed?

- How are the implemented (as distinct from declared) values at the top of this organization likely to affect the polarization of wealth and poverty in the societies where it operates?

- Does our corporate behaviour exemplify long-term thinking? Or does it support a society of short-term horizons, in which consumption now, regardless of its impact later, is the common priority, with little thought given to problems being created for future generations?

If you find that the answers to these questions are unsatisfactory to you, maybe you could give some thought as to how your influence as an organization could encourage a more ethical climate in the societies where it is at work.

ETHICAL PERFORMANCE AND CORPORATE GOVERNANCE

Corporate governance has been a major issue in many countries of the Western world in recent years. In the UK the government appointed Sir Adrian Cadbury to consider the matter. Changes in how companies operate at the top, and how they report their activities and performance, have resulted. Sir Richard Greenbury was later asked to address questions of public concern about top-level financial rewards. The London Stock Exchange has altered its rules to take account of many of their recommendations on company reporting, and indeed has made these semi-compulsory for listed companies (with an option of explaining

142 Ethics in Organizations

non-compliance). In Canada the Toronto Stock Exchange also tightened its rules, and the Senate of the Canadian government has been carrying out an inquiry amid many concerns about corporate scandal.

Not only in governmental circles but also in think-tanks and pressure groups this has been a serious theme throughout the early and mid-1990s. The subject is approached by different bodies from very different directions, and with different aspirations. Experts and activists in the field might variously wish to:

- Control perceived excesses in the rewarding of top managers.

- Provide better information on performance and risks.

- Increase attention to corporate social responsibility.

- Restore power to shareholders, including the small investors.

- Reduce the influence of transnational corporations.

- Control and eliminate fraud and corruption.

- Correct the alleged short-termism of the financial markets.

Each of these agenda items is influenced by whether the person or body concerned sees the organization primarily as a social organizm meeting the human needs of the many, or an impersonal mechanism for financial processing, creating wealth for the few. Too often positions polarize on that spectrum, with little recognition that any organization, business or otherwise, as it matures must develop multiple strands within its purpose. It inevitably leaves behind its old simplicity and must learn to live with complex ambiguities and dilemmas.

Thoughts of return to primitive simplicity, to a single measurement criterion, to a monolithic view of stakeholding, can only lead to long-term failure. The charitable organization concerned only about its effectiveness must now learn to be efficient. The thrusting, entrepreneurial single-location business now operating around the globe must learn to be responsive to multiple cultures and responsible toward people of many nationalities. The organization created by a single inspirational leader must recognize that its real wealth is in the skill of thousands of servicing staff in the junior ranks. The professional partnership which made a few families rich over several generations must learn that true 'ownership' now rests with the commitment and drive of professionals in the middle, without whom there is no business.

All of these impact on issues of governance. Some of the key points addressed by the Cadbury and Greenbury reports are listed in the box below. Developments so far have begun to touch some of the more outstanding public concerns, but much more can be expected as the new millennium approaches. What is more, these will not merely be matters of technique and procedure, but changes of profound ethical and practical significance.

Some Key Points from Cadbury and Greenbury

Clear division of responsibilities at the top.

Independency of non-executive directors.

Directors' responsibilities for effectiveness of internal control systems.

Effective audit committees.

Non-executive remuneration committees.

Genuinely demanding criteria for directors' performance-related pay.

WHAT ABOUT ETHICAL AUDITING?

Ethical audit is a powerful technique which has become more frequently used in recent years. Probably the best known example of its use in the UK is The Body Shop, which makes available detailed audit reports to the general public. Along with these reports, which are largely produced by independent external auditors, they include an explanation of their philosophy and methodology of audit. This is a company which is 'values-driven' in a way that very few commercial organizations can claim. It has much in common with voluntary organizations in that its formation was the consequence of a set of beliefs (whereas most companies attempt to articulate some beliefs or values after many years of operation). Because it is founded on very explicit values, the Body Shop audit process can be carried out with a clear sense of purpose and determination to act on the findings.

Before launching on an audit exercise there are many points to consider carefully. Seven are listed and discussed briefly here.

1. *Purpose* – be clear about the purpose, and therefore the scope, of the audit. Do you want to audit in order to obtain information which will help you steer the ethical development of the organization? Or to persuade critics that you're not as bad as they say? Or to follow a current fashion in management (sadly not uncommon with new methodologies)? Or to meet demands from a customer, or a client, or a regulator, or an owner?

2. *Type and topics* – what kind of audit do you want to carry out? The box below shows some of the options. If you have not clarified its purpose you won't be able to choose rationally between these. How will you determine what topics to include, and whether to start with a small subset the first time? Will you keep to auditing compliance with the rule book, or attitudes toward corporate environmental impact, or under-standing of health hazards? Or do you want to explore in depth the values of your people relative to all your major categories of stakeholder?

3. *Context* – in what managerial context is it being carried out? Is the organization accustomed to audits for other purposes? Is there commitment from the top to act on the findings? What pressures are there, and will there be, to do so?

4. *Process* – what process will you use? Will it be paper-based, using questionnaires? If so, do you have access to expert questionnaire design skills? (It is not difficult to design a meaningless questionnaire; there are many pitfalls.) Will it include technical assessments, and do you have access to the skills and equipment needed? Will it include face-to-face interviews? Especially for sensitive topics and areas of operation, do you have experienced interviewers?

5. *People* – be careful not to use only specialists in ethics. You need people who can communicate in language intelligible to the people they're working with. If you have carried out employee attitude surveys and climate studies in the past you probably have people with the necessary experience. If you have organization and management development specialists they will probably be at the heart of this exercise, as it could need to lead to substantial change programmes. If you use consultants, decide whether you want technicians to produce measurements and assessments, or change catalysts to help you transform the organization. Try not to use ethicists

without human-factors audit experience; conversely not auditors without adequate background in ethics (unless, of course, for a specific technical facet of ethical performance such as specialist aspects of environmental or health and safety ethics).

6. *Analysis and reporting* – do you have the capacity to process the data yourselves? Or will you use an outside agency? How will the various levels of report be produced, approved and published?

7. *Follow-up* – what follow-up do you intend? Clearly, you can't know exactly what will be required, but do you have at least outline plans for discussing and developing action programmes? To conduct an audit raises expectations. If you have accepted people's cooperation in the conduct of the audit you will be betraying a trust if you subsequently do nothing about the findings.

Ethical Audit? Many Varieties
Make sure you know what you want/need

Audit of policies and procedures (existence).

Audit of policies and procedures (compliance).

Audit of actual performance (external impact).

Audit of staff perceptions.

Audit of staff aspirations/concerns.

Audit of customer and other stakeholder perceptions.

Audit of customer and other stakeholder aspirations/concerns.

Audit of specific issues or problem areas.

Audit of legislative/regulatory compliance.

Audit comparison with reference scales, peers or benchmarks.

Useful References

The Body Shop (1995) *Values Report 1995*, five parts, including: *The Body Shop Approach to Ethical Auditing*, The Body Shop, Littlehampton. Also available on the World Wide Web at: http://www.think-act-change.com

Jonathan Charkham (1994) *Keeping Good Company: A study of corporate governance in five countries*, Oxford.

Robert Monks and Nell Minow (1991) *Power and Accountability*, Harper Collins, London.

Corporate Governance: An International Review, quarterly journal published by Blackwell.

Andrea Westall (ed) (1996) *Competitiveness and Corporate Governance*, Institute for Public Policy Research, London.

Part 3
Ideas for Progress

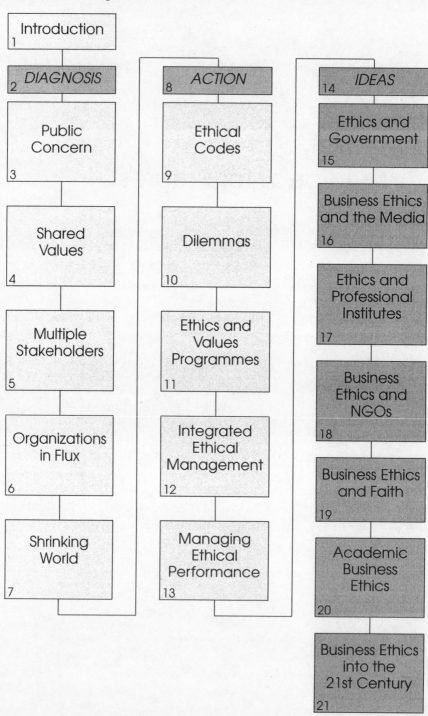

Introduction
1

DIAGNOSIS
2

Public
Concern
3

Shared
Values
4

Multiple
Stakeholders
5

Organizations
in Flux
6

Shrinking
World
7

ACTION
8

Ethical
Codes
9

Dilemmas
10

Ethics and
Values
Programmes
11

Integrated
Ethical
Management
12

Managing
Ethical
Performance
13

IDEAS
14

Ethics and
Government
15

Business Ethics
and the Media
16

Ethics and
Professional
Institutes
17

Business
Ethics and
NGOs
18

Business Ethics
and Faith
19

Academic
Business
Ethics
20

Business Ethics
into the
21st Century
21

Overview of Part 3

What does the future hold for business ethics? What will be the challenges? From where will come the pressures for change? Before devoting time to this question in Chapter 21 we look first at some of the already available sources both of challenge and assistance. These all provide useful information for the student of business ethics and for the activist who (whether inside or outside of industry) wishes to understand the issues in depth and gain some balance by exploring a range of perspectives. Such bodies also have their own ethical obligations and we will not neglect these. A newspaper, for example, may perform a valuable public service in exposing a fraudulent contract in the local government offices. The paper itself, however, also has a moral obligation to be balanced and fair, and to place truth before circulation-boosting sensation.

Governments

Governments enshrine some ethical imperatives in law, while leaving other issues to voluntary regulation and to a common sense of decency and responsibility. En route to making such judgements they frequently sponsor public debate of the issues. Discussion documents, the more serious official (as distinct from party-political) speeches and announcements, conference papers, etc., can be of great value to the corporate ethicist who wishes to review both the facts and the decisions.

Chapter 15 looks also at the ethics of governments themselves, whether they can be trusted, the values and codes of public life, and what is being done in many countries around the world in attempts to rebuild people's confidence in their governing institutions. The major components of a national integrity framework are outlined, these being of particular importance in countries which are in process of transition to participative democracy and market economics. Also, business people are not forgotten; there is a checklist of questions regarding relationships between private organizations and public institutions.

Media and Other Information Sources

The value of media freedoms to a civilised society are stressed. The media frequently report and sometimes investigate in depth the conduct of business organizations – often responsibly, although not always. Also, as the electronic communications revolution takes hold new sources of instant information are rapidly becoming available; we look at some of these and how to use them. This is designed as a practical chapter, including guidance on how to obtain and manage information from both traditional and modern electronic sources.

Professions

Professional and industry associations generally seek to establish minimum standards of conduct for their members, with varying degrees of regulation and policing. Chapter 17 is based on a survey of professional codes which I carried out in 1992. Such codes vary widely in their nature and impact.

Some professions are currently paying great attention to ethics, especially those in which technological advance threatens to outstrip our understanding of the implications for humanity and society. Medical ethics and bio-ethics are two closely related examples. Then there is the area of computing and information technologies, which generate a steady flow of moral concerns as the information age moves from dream to reality.

Voluntary Organizations

Voluntary organizations (frequently described in somewhat negative terms as) 'non-governmental organizations' or NGOs) often exert pressure on businesses in connection with their own particular interests and agendas. Some now exist with aspects of business ethics as their prime concern. In the next chapter I argue that confrontation between pressure groups and companies, while sometimes inevitable in the context of specific incidents, should not be the norm. More progress would be made if the two sides talked and attempted to understand one another. The American example of the Coalition for Environmentally Responsible Economies is explored to illustrate a gradual movement toward working together with greater understanding on all sides.

Faith

Churches and other religious bodies frequently comment on business matters, especially when they feel that people, either as individuals or communities, are being treated less well than is desirable; an increasing number give serious long-term and well-informed thought to questions of the relationship between faith and working life. Chapter 19 describes some recent, and some not so recent, initiatives, some within the boundaries of individual faiths and others involving representatives of different faiths working together.

Academia

Colleges and universities now pay much more attention than in the past to the moral implications of business policy and professional conduct. A large number now have specialist units with this as either the sole or prime topic of study. Many MBA programmes include ethics or corporate social responsibility as an important theme, something almost unheard of even five years ago. High quality journals are now produced on both sides of the Atlantic; conferences (local, national and international) proliferate. There are both strengths and weaknesses in this academic trend.

Ethics in the Influencing Bodies

Each of these bodies, as well as commenting on and prescribing for the business world, has ethical issues within its own operation. We will look at some of these and encourage managers within them to take a serious view of their own ethical standards, on the argument that those who seek to guide, advise or legislate for others should pay attention to themselves also.

This is not, of course, to demand that a person or organization must be 100 per cent safe from any fear of accusation before commenting on behaviour elsewhere in society. In that case this book could never have been written. I cannot lay claim to perfection any more than the next person. It seems fair, however, to call for honesty, equity, objectivity, reasonableness and understanding, especially on the part of those who set themselves up to criticize. It seems reasonable to demand balanced and thoughtful, courteous and respectful, as well as provocative and challenging, behaviour on the part of all who make moral demands on the businesses which deliver the relative comfort and prosperity from which they themselves benefit.

In brief, this third part of the book is about (i) how such bodies currently contribute their critiques and ideas, and (ii) how they might examine themselves, and in doing so bring even greater advantages to business society in the future.

The 21st Century

What is around the corner? We can only know to a limited extent. We can extrapolate from present experience and make intelligent guesses, but we can never be certain. One thing we can be fairly certain of, though, is that as technologies and societies develop they will give rise to ever more complex moral dilemmas. Managers in organizations need to be prepared for these. There is grave danger in an attitude to technology which implies, 'If it can be done it must be done'. Choices about the application of technology, and about transitions in world society, are made at all levels from the major global players to the single small-town individual. Ethics as a skill, and values as a foundation, must be given far higher priority in the training of coming generations of leaders, managers and professional specialists, indeed of everyone.

15

Ethics and Government

One of the prime responsibilities of a government must be to build an environment of justice, of transparency, and of trust. No economy can function efficiently without trust. Government itself, in the long term if not immediately, must fail if it does not carry public confidence. In a democratic society, if public officials are to be capable of taking delegated powers effectively from parliament and government there must be two-way trust. Ministers suffer constant distraction from their executive and legislative priorities as journalists and others demand statements and explanations about relative trivia and incipient scandals when there is not an atmosphere of trust in their general honesty and integrity. Governments around the world have in recent years been paying considerable attention to ethical standards.

A government can usefully make four main kinds of contribution to cause of ethical improvement in business and in other organizations of society. It can:

- set an example by the transparently blameless conduct of its own affairs;

- legislate for, regulate, and police the conduct of organizations (with international cooperation where needed);

- encourage organizations to adopt effective voluntary codes of conduct without the heavy hand of legislation; and

- stimulate national (and where appropriate, international) debate on moral aspects of government and the life of society as a whole.

CAN GOVERNMENTS BE TRUSTED?

Around the world governments and public administrators face crises of confidence. In the United States a recent poll in one state (Arizona) showed that 71 per cent of respondents believed that lawmakers would accept bribes if they were offered. This poll was taken shortly after a highly publicized scandal, but polls in other states have shown not dissimilar results. In the UK a 1993 MORI poll showed that when asked whether they would generally trust various categories of people to tell the truth, whereas 80 per cent of the respondents considered that clergymen would do so, the score for politicians in general was only 14 per cent, almost as low as journalists (10 per cent).

As one reads official surveys and reports one can only be struck by the basic similarity of the concerns from country to country. In the UK, just as this book is being finalized, there is a public outcry about the pay of members of Parliament. Following the recommendations of an independent inquiry they have accepted a pay increase in the region of eight or ten times those paid recently to other workers in Britain. The fact that they have been seriously underpaid for many years is widely ignored. The message of many newspapers is about 'fat cat' politicians. The issue of pay in public service is not unique to Britain; in the United States it has also been a debating point for many years.

Public Concerns – the Ethics of Government, Members of Parliament and Officials

Lobbying and lobbyists.

Relationships between ministers and officials.

Conflicts of Interest – operation of the register of interests.

'Cash for questions' – payment for asking parliamentary questions.

Employment after leaving office.

Outside employment of Members of Parliament ('second jobs').

Boundary between work for government and work for party.

MPs working as parliamentary consultants.

Whether it be a public argument over pay or an isolated instance of corruption, both elected representatives and appointed officials face a public climate of distrust not in any way helped by the less responsible elements in the media (press, radio and television) who appear at times to enjoy nothing better than the sport of tearing down and discrediting people in the public eye. Sometimes journalists' courageous exposure of genuine wrongdoing is a valuable public service. However, in countries where public administration is by and large honest the constant barrage of accusation and innuendo can easily become counterproductive. Faced with this kind of negative media attention both politicians and officials face an uphill task of building credibility, but it has to be done.

The emphases vary around the world. In some countries it may be the conduct of elections; in the United States the issue of controlling campaign contributions has a high profile in some states. Elsewhere it may be corruption, for example associated with East European privatization programmes. In African countries it may be nepotism, in Italy the bribery of legislators and tax authorities. In many countries, whistleblowing and the protection of those who have the courage to speak out about malpractice have been high on the public agenda. In England the relationship between lobbyists and elected Parliamentarians was one of the principal elements in the 'sleaze' accusations which led to Prime Minister John Major in 1994 appointing Lord Nolan to lead a Committee on Standards in Public Life.

The Josephson Principles of Public Service Ethics

Public office as public trust.

Independent objective judgement.

Accountability.

Democratic leadership.

Respectability and fitness for public office.

PRINCIPLES AND CODES

The box above shows the titles of the five 'Principles of public service ethics' promoted by the Government Ethics Center of the Joseph & Edna Josephson Institute based in Marina del Rey, California. Lord Nolan, in his 1995 report, 'Standards in public life', adopted a list of 'Seven principles of public life', shown in the box overleaf.

Lord Nolan's report also called for the formulation of codes of conduct for different groups of public servants (elected and appointed), building on the seven basic principles and applying them to the specific demands and circumstances of different roles. As an example, his report gave a draft code for Members of Parliament, covering general principles and financial interests.

The Seven Principles of Public Life

Selflessness.

Integrity.

Objectivity.

Accountability.

Openness.

Honesty.

Leadership.

(The Nolan Committee, 1995)

This provision of a foundation of basic principles is a considerable step forward from (for example) the codes of conduct for the National Health Service some months earlier. In Chapter 9 I recommended that an organization should start from its purpose, move to the principles of behaviour, and then expand these into material referring in greater detail to critical areas of practice. The NHS documents jump straight to practice, making them of very limited use outside the specific areas of activity referred to. A code based on clearly articulated general principles is a far more powerful tool. (Although here I list only the key words of Lord Nolan's 'seven principles', his report provides a one or two sentence elaboration of each principle.)

ETHICS TRAINING AND LEADERSHIP

As already indicated, many other governments have introduced ethics initiatives in recent years. In 1989 the United States federal government enacted the Ethics Reform Act, strengthening conflict-of-interest rules and increasing the requirements for financial disclosure. In 1992 the United States Office of the Comptroller General reported on a review of various aspects of employment practice in the federal workforce. The report expressed concern at problems of public image, and although acknowledging some beneficial impact of ethics reform legislation identified lack of commitment among top management and shortcomings in training as two of the reasons why more progress had not been made. In particular it reported that almost three-quarters of the staff surveyed were unaware of the protections offered by the whistleblower legislation to people who reported misconduct.

This subject of ethics training was mentioned repeatedly in a report of the Auditor General to the Canadian House of Commons in May 1995. In nine departments surveyed, less than 6 per cent of staff had received ethics-related training. It called for training which 'provided information on ethical values and formal rules in government' and would 'provide public servants with the tools to deal with ethically questionable requests... [and] ethical dilemmas'. Wisely, it concluded also that the enhancement of ethics in government is not a matter of quick and easy initiatives and programmes, but of long-term sustained effort. It shares the requirements of continuous improvement programmes in the field of service quality – the need must be communicated clearly and repeatedly, and both promoted and exemplified from the very top. Only if the stated ethical principles are seen to be implemented in everyday decisions at senior levels can it be expected that people in more junior positions will take it seriously. Leadership is crucial.

In discussing ethics training, a task force of the (US) National Conference of State Legislatures in its 1995 report, 'Strengthening State Legislatures', called for programmes to be designed for lawmakers, staff, also lobbyists; these should take legal requirements as a minimum and emphasize 'the importance of avoiding even the appearance of impropriety'. This is in marked contrast to newspaper reports from one state where, allegedly, lobbyists had been provided with training – but conducted by lobbyists for lobbyists, with at least some of the content consisting of guidance on how to find loopholes in the rules!

NATIONAL INTEGRITY FRAMEWORK

The examples given above have all been from advanced Western societies where, in general, while admitting that lapses do occur, there are already quite high standards of behaviour in the governmental systems. Transparency International, however, works extensively with countries where this is not the case. Its *National Integrity Systems Source Book* outlines the basic components for systems of government which aspire to a high degree of morality and transparency.

Although adapted considerably, the following list was derived originally from points noted during a reading of that document while I was working with TI in Slovakia and Romania:

- Transparently honest election processes.

- Open and fair parliamentary structures, processes and procedures.

- Rules to counter conflict of interest in public life.

- Public bureaucracies with values of public service.

- Public servants adequately paid.

- Administrative law ensuring accountability of decision makers.

- Effective public audit processes.

- Independent judiciary.

- Transparent and competitive public procurement processes.

- Free press, both challenging and responsible.

- Independent organizations of civil society.

The Hungarian ethicist Laszlo Zolnai has argued that for long-term survival an economic and political system must possess three characteristics: legality, morality and legitimacy. The last of these will be determined substantially by the first two. Governments do well to take great care in cultivating the public reputation of their principal institutions – and not by the manipulation of popular opinion but by practical demonstration of the highest standards of conduct.

National Integrity – Seven Vital Strands

Whether one is working with a governmental body in a society with existing generally high standards (seeking to improve further, or to prevent slippage) or in a setting routinely characterized by serious abuses, there are certain elements in a development programme which virtually everyone working in the field has found to be critical. These are listed here (and they appear in different formats in several places throughout this book) as seven vital strands of ethics development. Constructing a national integrity framework, and building governmental institutions to support it, is not merely a matter of having the mechanics of legislation and procedure in place. It is about the hearts and minds of people. It is a long-term project of many years during which there will be many periods of regression before further advance is apparently made. The seven, therefore, have a number eight.

1. Leadership – committed, visible, consistent.

2. Code – purpose and principles, with rules of practice.

3. Training – for all affected, public servants and others.

4. Ethics officers – to champion an improvement process.

5. Whistleblowing – safe routes to report serious wrongdoing.

6. Audit – stressing problems and progress, not blame.

7. Positive publicity – promoting integrity and service.

8. *Determination, persistence and hope.*

CHALLENGES TO BUSINESS

Given that the majority of people reading this book will probably be interested primarily in ethical development in business organizations, what does all of the above have to say to them? The box below contains a number of questions which, if taken seriously, will be searching. Some may consider them naive. Others will recognize them as addressing important aspects of corporate social responsibility. Over the past two centuries companies have acquired a considerable number of privileges. The idea of making it possible for an organization to become an 'economic person', with rights under law, and limited liability, developed slowly over many years. Although these rights (going far beyond those of individuals) are generally taken for granted in this modern age, they are not an inevitable part of nature, but are an artificial construct introduced for the public good. Strong forces are constantly at work to reduce their obligations still further, usually on the argument that what is good for the economy is good for everyone. The box overleaf includes some counter-balancing challenges.

Challenges – Naive or Necessary?

If your business is a supplier to government or other public bodies, how honest are you in your bidding for contracts?

Do you make illicit payments at any level in order to influence the choice of supplier?

If your business is a beneficiary of government pro-grammes, such as regional development aid or other forms of grant, do you provide accurate information or, where estimates are required, your honest best judge-ments?

In entering returns for taxation purposes, are you scrupulously honest, using whatever legal allowances exist to best advantage but never dishonestly avoiding taxes?

In your dealings with lawmakers, whether elected representatives or senior policy officials, do you seek to move the formulation of legislation in your favour through improper influence or by means of financial or other inducements rather than by rational argument?

In your organization is there an attitude that only conven-ient laws will be kept; otherwise the art is to avoid being caught out?

Is your attitude to government one of seeking to keep all legislation and regulation well away from the business world, so as to allow business to have a free rein with minimal obligations to society?

Has your business ever required its executives to consider the 'Seven principles of public service', and to ask what impact these should have on their dealings with public servants?

LEGISLATION AND/OR REGULATION

We have already considered some areas in which governments might legislate for improved standards of behaviour. These, however, were primarily in the context of improving its own standards – although the concept of a 'National integrity framework' extends to cover all sectors of society.

Governments vary, sometimes out of pragmatism, sometimes out of political principle, in the degree to which they wish to legislate for the behaviour of business and other organizations. In most developed countries all parties would consider it appropriate to have basic legislation covering such matters as monopoly (or 'antitrust' to give the American term), anti-competitive practices, various forms of financial fraud, environmental protection and basic rules on employment conditions, to name but a few.

When legislation is first introduced in a new field it tends to be treated as a moral issue. Very often there is enthusiastic (sometimes doctrinaire) campaigning on all sides of the argument. After a number of years, although the details may still be under dispute from time to time, topics come to be treated as 'natural' areas for legislation. The debates about the dividing line between morality, social fashion and law tend to arise in the context of new issues.

TAMING THE NET

One of the areas in which this debate is going on at present is the control of content on the 'Information super-highway', the Internet. The debate is often centred around the imposition of national pornography laws, especially as parents become concerned about what might be readily available to their children via their modems, outside the usual forms of parental control, the dispensing of money and the allowance of time and travel outside the home. In fact, however, there are much wider issues ranging from material which explicitly incites to racial hatred to questions of honest and fair trading now that it is possible to conduct commercial business over the Net.

The United States federal government introduced its Communications Decency Act against an uproar of objections from many sections of the on-line community. Legal wrangling over its constitutional validity are likely to go on for many years. The British approach is to tread more carefully. It is considered by many police experts that the Internet, because of its internationally distributed nature and its lack of single ownership or control, is virtually unpoliceable. This does not, however, mean that nothing can be controlled. Existing legislation is considered to be adequate to cover extremes of violence and perversions such as paedophilia. Otherwise, protection of children is seen as something that will be best assured by a combination of advice to parents and teachers, the use of protective software, a possible content-classification scheme, and a voluntary Code of Practice adopted by a new industry body, The Internet Service Providers Association. Its major topics are listed in the box below. The Code is intended to be voluntary for the first year from May 1996, and then to become obligatory for all members of the Association.

The new code is relatively mild in its terms, but there is a strong libertarian movement within the Net community which will continue campaigning for total lack of legal or regulatory restraint, whether voluntary or otherwise. The American John Barlow has probably gone further than most in drafting in early 1995 his 'Declaration of the Independence of Cyberspace'. In it he announces to governments around the world, 'I declare the global social space we are building to be naturally independent of the tyrannies you seek to impose on us.'

Topics covered by the Code of Practice of the Internet Service Providers Association

Legality – 'not contain anything which is in breach of the law, nor omit anything which the law requires'.

Decency – 'violence, sadism, cruelty, or racial hatred… not used to promote or facilitate prostitution'.

Honesty – 'services and promotional material… (not) inaccuracy, ambiguity, exaggeration, omission or otherwise'.

Data protection – the Data Protection Registrar, and other data users.

Fair trading – consumers, other businesses… complaints procedure.

This may be an extreme position which will not prove tenable in most countries, but the debate about freedom of expression on a global network will not go away. Its global nature is the critical issue. Resolving the tension between, on the one hand, controlling the worst and most socially dangerous excesses and, on the other, avoiding a situation in which any illiberal, totalitarian government might dictate what (for example, political or religious) material can be placed on the World Wide Web, will continue to challenge the minds of ethicists and legislators for a long time to come.

STIMULATING A MORAL DEBATE

The UK government did not arrive at its position on Internet content control quickly or lightly, nor did it do so without an extensive consultation process. In fact, it used the very technology that it was concerned with as a medium for an important part of its consultation. Discussion forums (known as Collaborative Open Groups, or COGs) were established on the Internet to debate this and related topics, the forums being open to all comers. One of these COGs was known as 'The Ethics COG' and was initially set up following a parliamentary question, tabled by the Labour MP for Leeds West, John Battle, on the availability of pornography on the Internet, although it was given a wider brief than that: 'To look at the ethical issues arising from the use of the Internet. These include the distribution of undesirable material, the misuse of Internet facilities such as electronic mail, and any other related aspects of Internet use.' After several months of sometimes vigorous exchange between around 80 participants, a summary report to ministers was developed in mid-1995.

Others of the almost 20 COGs considered issues such as the use of the information superhighways in education, by women, by families, and by the disabled.

It has to be said that in recent years the British government has not, by and large, been successful in broadening the debate on national morality. Its 1993/94 'Back to basics' debate foundered on the rocks of party politics, and possibly also on a too narrow definition of its subject matter. In many circles, to introduce the subject of morality is met with an assumption that one is about to advocate the reintroduction of '19th century values', whatever they might be. And yet the debate is of great importance. As the post-communist economies of East and Central Europe have discovered, a society has to be built on shared values. An economy cannot operate efficiently without trust. To ensure that these issues are debated, and that their implications are widely understood, is a vital role of government along with other leading institutions in society.

Useful References

Canadian Government (1995) *Ethics and Fraud Awareness in Government*; report of the Auditor General to the (Canadian) House of Commons.

HM Government (1995) *CCTA Report on Information Superhighways – July 1995*, published by the UK government at: http://www.open.gov.uk/ccta/cctapubs.htm

The Joseph and Edna Josephson Institute of Ethics (1990) *Preserving the Public Trust: Principles of Public Service Ethics*; Government Ethics Center, Marina del Rey, CA.

Lord Nolan (1995) *Standards in Public Life*; First Report of the Committee on Standards in Public Life, Chairman Lord Nolan, HMSO, London.

TI (1996) *National Integrity Systems: The TI Source Book*; Transparency International, Berlin.

16

Business Ethics and the Media

(NOTE: This chapter includes a number of references to the Internet and the World Wide Web. Even a year ago it would have been appropriate to provide basic explanation and instructions. Given that the Web is now used regularly by a substantial proportion of professionals in most fields of endeavour, addresses for Web pages are given more or less like telephone numbers. Just about everyone knows how to use a telephone. Increasingly, professional people know how to use the various types of service on the Internet and proprietary electronic services.)

Being a journalist can be a hazardous business. According to the 1995 report of the New York-based organization, the Committee to Protect Journalists, more than 180 journalists were in prison in 22 countries at the end of the year. More than 50 had been killed in the line of duty during the year, and only six of these were in combat zones. The assassination of journalists is a serious problem around the world. Baroness Chalker, the British Minister for Overseas Development referred in a speech to Commonwealth heads of government in November 1995 to a report from Freedom House, also based in New York, stating that ten countries of the Commonwealth fell into the lowest of their three categories of press freedom. Many of us in countries where the press are almost totally unfettered often fail to appreciate the advantages that we have over parts of the world where freedom of expression is a distant, often seemingly unrealistic, hope somewhere over the horizon.

In the business world, however, press freedom is sometimes seen as a mixed blessing. Too often journalists get stories wrong, either in fact or interpretation, and cause damage to corporate reputations. And yet, without freedom of investigation and reporting, many episodes of scandalous behaviour would not have been uncovered, and many people would continue to be cheated and robbed by the unscrupulous.

In this chapter we will look first at positive and constructive ways in which the media can be used by those of us who study business and professional ethics. Toward the end of the chapter we will turn to consider ethical issues in journalism itself. Some who, like me, greatly value the institution of a free press nevertheless feel entitled periodically to call for higher standards in this important profession. Freedom must not be abused.

USING PRINTED NEWS MEDIA IN BUSINESS ETHICS

For someone starting to study business ethics, and wanting to ensure that the study is rooted in practical realities rather than solely in theory, the serious newspapers provide a readily available source of material. Reports containing relevant information will include such items as:

- court cases and tribunal hearings;
- journalists' crusading investigations;
- consumer watchdog documents and comment;
- industrial accidents;
- pressure-group campaigns;
- official enquiries.

Whether kept as cuttings or solely as references, these should be filed in some systematic manner. Over the years I have used various combinations of the following:

- A box of filing cards (old-fashioned maybe, but still very effective – blank cards are easily carried in an envelope, a jacket pocket or a small bag).
- An alphabetically-indexed pocket notebook.
- A pocket electronic organizer or palmtop computer.
- A physical file of press-cuttings, indexed under date, topic or organization name.

Probably the most powerful tool for accumulating and analysing this kind of information is still an old piece of Lotus software called Lotus Agenda. Sadly it is no longer easily available, being DOS-based and never upgraded by its developers to a Windows version, but it has powers of sifting, searching, relating and assembling text entries that are, in the view of its fans, far beyond anything else on the market. It is easy not only to search for entries which have been deliberately labelled with keywords but also to assemble related items based on full text search, even including external text files linked to the entries.

This chapter is being typed on a palmtop computer (a Hewlett Packard 200LX) in a hotel room. On it I have a small database of press and magazine articles which I have come across while away from my desk. These are easily merged into an Agenda database back at the office. Use of a system such as this, whether electronic or on paper, very quickly accumulates a substantial amount of reference material as fuel for thought.

Of course, there are some cautionary comments to be added here. It is frequently observed by people who are close to newsworthy events that they rarely read press reports which tally with what they themselves have seen and heard; and yet, they say, 'I still tend to believe the reports of things that are new to me. Why am I so gullible?'

This is, of course, a somewhat unkind view of the press, but (sadly) is at times justified. If you intend to make a study of any incident in depth, try to get access to a variety of perspectives. Read reports from several newspapers, and monthlies of different political colours.

Not only the major national dailies are useful sources, but also the regional, provincial and local press. In reviewing the Archbishop of Canterbury's July 1996 call in the House of Lords for national moral renewal I found it valuable to obtain the perspective of a Welsh newspaper as well as the English press. In examining a bribery scandal in the Ministry of Defence, I obtained a better insight into the impact on real, living people by reading the discussion in a local evening daily from an area of the country where many employees of a major contractor had lost their jobs as a consequence of the scandal.

SPECIALIST ETHICS PUBLICATIONS

In addition to the general printed media there are, of course, specialist journals. The quarterly *Business Ethics: a European Review* is edited by Professor Jack Mahoney of the London Business School. It is outstanding for its quality of material, in jargon-free English, drawing on writers from all over Europe and from across the Atlantic.

Of the several specialist North American publications my own favourite is the *Journal of Business Ethics* edited largely by a team from various Canadian universities. This is substantially more academic in tone than Jack Mahoney's European journal but the majority of its papers are easily accessible to the non-specialist reader, and the editors are to be congratulated on selecting papers which have something useful to say to practitioners as well as to fellow researchers.

USING THE ELECTRONIC MEDIA

An amazing transformation in global information availability has been brought about in recent years first by the fax machine and then (even more revolutionary) by the development of e-mail and the Internet, especially the World Wide Web.

In Chapter 20, on the academic input to business ethics, I will look at several ways in which specialist institutes and associations are using the Web to communicate and to exchange ideas. Here I am concerned with using electronic media for news gathering.

Many traditional business magazines and journals now have electronic editions, frequently for a subscription but also in many cases providing a limited selection of articles free of charge. *Fortune*, for example, now publishes its annual corporate reputation survey on its Web pages. This has within it several aspects of reputation with a significant ethical dimension. The survey is open to the criticism that it focuses primarily on those aspects of reputation which might be expected to carry most weight with the stock market and institutional investors rather than with society at large. Having said this, it is the most serious survey of its type. Interestingly, the 1996 survey reports that some top US executives now have their company's reputation ranking built into the determination of their annual incentive plan.

It is not only the major business journals and the high-profile international newspapers such as the *Financial Times* which have Web pages. Even in some of the developing economies of post-communist Central and Eastern Europe a significant number of papers have English language editions, and some now place highlights from the news on Web pages, even archiving these for future reference with keyword and free-text search software. There are also many on-line news services associated with the big electronic information service providers. CompuServe, for example, gives access to ENS, an electronic news service which allows one to collect into folders the stories from wire services such as Reuters and Associated Press containing the words or phrases which you specify. By this means one can be ahead even of the daily papers (although it takes some practice to develop the skill needed to avoid being inundated with unwanted stories about, for example, a floor polish manufacturer when you really want to read about Poland and the Polish). Incidentally, this was the method used to collect most of the information in the opening paragraphs of Chapter 2.

Also on the Web is to be found a wide range of government official documents, announcements and press releases. The United States government is very good at this, and others including the UK are developing this service rapidly. Example sources for an Eastern European search are shown in the box below.

Example of addresses used in a search for a Privatization ethics study

BULGARIAN TELEGRAPH AGENCY (BTA) index, mostly from the Bulgarian Embassy in Washington:
http://www.hri.org/news/agencies/bta/

BULGARIAN NEWS ARCHIVE – electronic news sources:
http://asudesign.eas.asu.edu/places/Bulgaria/news/

US Embassies' LATEST CABLES from CEE countries:
http://www.itaiep.doc.gov/eebic/cable.html

CORRUPTION RISKS IN THE PRIVATIZATION PROCESS (by Ivan Miklos, former privatization minister, Slovakia):
http://savba.savba.sk/logos/journals/ap/miklos1.html

Included in these are embassy communications. The US foreign service makes public some of its embassy telegrams, which include economic news and comment. The example address given is for the US Embassy in Sofia. Also shown is the address for pages from the Bulgarian Telegraph Agency. I was interested in ethical issues in the Bulgarian privatization process and could access, search and download a wide variety of information from sources like these, including electronic newspapers.

At the start of this chapter it was stated that this book would not give a guide to using the Internet. There is one practical tip, however, that is highly relevant here. Many of these news-source organizations are acquiring the habit (a bad one in my opinion) of installing fancy, multicolour designs in their opening pages, which then take for ever to transmit. The first time you access one of them you have little choice but to travel this route. Once you have penetrated behind the front page, however, and arrived at the information you really want – such as a news archive catalogue, which will usually be in text form without much in the way of fancy graphics – enter this address into your browser's bookmark list so that next time you want to go there you can miss out the time-consuming front-end.

SEARCHING THE WEB

What about other information available electronically? Below are some addresses of useful official sites. A great deal is also now published by NGOs and professional organizations around the world, including much that might otherwise be difficult to access. I recently wanted to collect quickly some material on the ethics of scientific research. It took approximately three minutes to find a most useful report placed on the Web by the National Sciences and Engineering Research Council of Canada. It described in some detail a 1994 by-invitation conference of senior Canadian researchers and research administrators in Toronto on 'The challenges of academic integrity in a rapidly changing environment' – exactly what I was looking for. In researching this chapter the information in the opening paragraphs about the hazards of journalism came from a speculative search using 'Alta Vista', as did my introduction to the Society of Professional Journalists whose code is quoted at the end of the chapter.

SOME USEFUL OFFICIAL SITES

UK Central/Local Government Document SEARCH facility:
http://www.open.gov.uk/search/search.htm

The European Commission:
http://europa.eu.int/en/comm.html

Business Information from the US Government:
http://www.itaiep.doc.gov/eebic/cduga.html

The World Bank:
http://www.worldbank.org/

OECD – try looking for 'bribery' using their search facility:
http://www.oecd.org/

What is Alta Vista? It is a publicly available Internet search facility designed and operated by Digital Equipment Corporation, and is one of a number of similar search engines – the addresses of some of which are given in the box below.

It is important always to use a multiplicity of sources. The media, of all types, print and electronic, are as flawed and biased as humans in general. Later in this chapter we will examine some of the ethical issues involved in journalism. For now let us make sure to remember, *caveat lector.*

Some World Wide Web Search facilities

ALTA VISTA: http://www.altavista.digital.com

EXCITE: http://www.excite.com/

LYCOS: http://www.lycos.com/

INPUT TO THE MEDIA

The media (radio, television and print) rely to a considerable degree on information provided to them. Many organizations regularly supply them with press releases and briefings, and some are only too ready in furthering their own interests to attempt manipulation, even distortion, of the news. I would argue that this does not in any way reduce the media obligation to seek accuracy, fairness and balance in their reporting. The excuse that, 'We can only go on what we're told', is simply not good enough. Having said that, they frequently do receive questionable input, and the organizations providing this cannot escape their own share of responsibility for misinforming the public.

I recently wanted to look at some of the ethical issues involved in the dispute between Greenpeace and Shell over the disposal of the Brent Spar oil storage platform in the North Sea. To start with I turned to the excellent (diskette and paper) package designed for schools by WWF (the World Wide Fund for Nature). It contains report summaries, correspondence, press releases, newspaper and scientific magazine articles along with other related data provided by both parties to the argument so as to allow students to examine the information for themselves and to arrive at their own conclusions rather than accepting at face value the frequently oversimplified analyses of the popular press and television.

My interest was less in the technical arguments about pollution, important as they are, but rather in how the protagonists had represented their respective cases to the public. By using several search engines on the Web it was possible to locate full-text copies of several of the key technical reports, including the independent audit of the contents of the rig and its pollution potential carried out by DNV (Det Norske Veritas) subsequent to Shell's decision to withdraw from its initial plan for deep-sea disposal.

The Ethics of Press Releases

Rather than comment on the findings of this study, opposite is an exercise for readers to carry out for themselves.

FURTHER THOUGHTS ON MEDIA ETHICS

We turn now to ways in which journalists can further the cause of well-behaved business, and then to their own standards of behaviour.

Journalism can be a help to business (indeed to politics, economics and society as a whole) if they take to heart the following six appeals:

Continue:

- to investigate wrongdoing, fairly and with balance;
- to challenge industry to work with determination to achieve higher standards of public responsibility;
- to seek out and to report good news, without feeling that a report is incomplete without a negative downside.

Cease:

- to bias or exaggerate stories in order to create sensational headlines;
- to seek personal stature by belittling or even destroying the reputations and careers of others;
- to confuse forceful interviewing with an urge to belittle or to discredit.

Journalists' organizations have codes of conduct in addition to those imposed by governmental or other statutory regulatory

Exercise

Read the DNV report (or at least its executive summary) and the DNV press release, then the press releases from both Shell and Greenpeace. Next, answer for yourself the following questions:

1. Having read the independent report, do the comments by the protagonists read as though they read the same document?

2. How fairly do the comments in each of the press releases reflect: (a) the overall thrust of the report, and (b) the balance of evidence for and against the issuing organizations' own positions?

World Wide Web addresses; documents on Brent Spar and the DNV independent report:

BRENT SPAR – Shell Web Pages
http://www.shellexpro.brentspar.com/index.html

BRENT SPAR – Greenpeace Web Pages
http://www.greenpeace.org/~comms/brent/brent.html

DNV Report, October 1995 – EXECUTIVE SUMMARY
http://www.shellexpro.brentspar.com/archive/dnv_rep/man_summ/1_summ.html

DNV Report – DNV Press release 18 Oct 95
http://www.shellexpro.brentspar.com/debate/shell_v/3_theway/33_incom/comm_2.html

DNV Report – Greenpeace Press Release 18 Oct 95
http://www.greenpeace.org/~comms/brent/oct18.html

DNV Report – Shell's news release 18 Oct 95
http://www.shellexpro.brentspar.com/debate/shell_v/3_theway/31_suk/1995/4a_news.html

bodies. As with other professions the real issue is not the mere existence of a code but the effectiveness or otherwise of processes to ensure its application. Not being a regulated profession in the sense that a practitioner can be struck off a register and legally barred from practising (as is the case in most developed countries, for example, with medical practitioners and lawyers) it is not easy to police any code. Capturing the hearts and minds of professional journalists and their editors would seem to be the key to the matter.

The Society of Professional Journalists, the leading professional body of journalists in the United States, has a code which when this chapter was initially written opened with the powerful statement that, 'The duty of journalists is to serve the truth.' The code has recently been revised, and still stresses truth, justice and respect for others. An extensive extract from the 1996 version is given here.

Extract from the Code of Ethics of the Society of Professional Journalists

Seek Truth and Report It

Journalists should be honest, fair and courageous in gathering, reporting and interpreting information.

Journalists should:

Test the accuracy of information from all sources and exercise care to avoid inadvertent error. Deliberate distortion is never permissible.

Diligently seek out subjects of news stories to give them the opportunity to respond to allegations of wrong-doing.

Identify sources wherever feasible. The public is entitled to as much information as possible on sources' reliability.

Always question sources' motives before promising anonymity. Clarify conditions attached to any promise made in exchange for information. Keep promises.

Make certain that headlines, news teases and promotional material, photos, video, audio, graphics, sound bites and quotations do not misrepresent. They should not oversimplify or highlight incidents out of context.

Never distort the content of news photos or video. Image enhancement for technical clarity is always permissible. Label montages and photo illustrations.

Avoid misleading re-enactments or staged news events. If re-enactment is necessary to tell a story, label it.

Avoid undercover or other surreptitious methods of gathering information except when traditional open methods will not yield information vital to the public. Use of such methods should be explained as part of the story.

Never plagiarise.

Tell the story of the diversity and magnitude of the human experience boldly, even when it is unpopular to do so.

Examine their own cultural values and avoid imposing those values on others.

Avoid stereotyping by race, gender, age, religion, geography, sexual orientation, disability, physical appearance or social status.

Support the open exchange of views, even views which they find repugnant.

Give voice to the voiceless; official and unofficial sources of information can be equally valid.

Distinguish between advocacy and news reporting. Analysis and commentary should be labelled and not misrepresent fact or context.

Distinguish news from advertising and shun hybrids that blur the lines between the two.

Recognise a special obligation to ensure that the public's business is conducted in the open and that government records are open to inspection.

Quoted with permission – Society of Professional Journalists (USA)

The new SPJ code includes four main sections with the following headings:

- Seek Truth and Report It
- Minimize Harm
- Act Independently
- Be Accountable.

At the beginning of the previous chapter, while discussing ethics in government, it was pointed out that a 1993 MORI poll in the United Kingdom showed that only 10 per cent of respondents considered that one could reasonably expect a journalist to be telling the truth. There is very clearly a great deal of ground for the profession to recover.

There are now probably more specialists in the ethics of journalism and the media than ever before. It is up to them to avoid the temptation to work at defending their profession and to get to grips with the difficult issues of accuracy, honesty and fairness in reporting. If society gladly gives freedom to its press, it has every right to demand total integrity in return.

Given high standards of reporting and knowledgeable interpretation, there is no reason why business organizations should fear the press. True, journalists may at times keep business people on their toes – but that is not necessarily a bad thing. With mutual respect each can benefit the other while maintaining total integrity.

17

Ethics and Professional Institutes

This chapter had its genesis in a small research exercise that I carried out in 1992. We wrote to 35 professional institutes asking whether they would be willing to let us have a copy of their professional code of practice, and eventually obtained 20 codes for analysis. Since then our collection of professional codes has grown, and we have worked with some institutes on matters relating to their principles and values. The conclusions from the original work still hold true, and are outlined here along with practical recommendations.

We wanted then to develop a set of working guidelines, based upon what we saw as the strengths and weaknesses of the codes we examined, and which we hoped would help institutes in the formulation and enhancement of their professional codes in the future. This is also the aim of the present chapter. To do this we aimed (a) to discover what themes were most commonly covered by the codes; (b) to examine their construction and presentation; and (c) to identify the types of procedure in place for ensuring compliance.

In Chapter 9 it was pointed out that most managers and professionals at least formally acknowledge allegiance to several codes – those of the membership-organizations to which they belong. In practice, however, many of these codes are little regarded. Within professional bodies themselves, however, there is now a much greater awareness. Many have in recent years revisited their codes and developed them to meet the changing needs and priorities of the 1990s. In particular many have been examining the need for more comprehensive reference to the natural environment.

The regulated professions such as medicine, accountancy and law have always been kept conscious of their ethical basis by the requirement to maintain discipline and to protect the public. In certain professions the ethical component comes naturally to the fore more than in others. This applies especially to the 'caring professions' where the human dimension of the service is prominent. The United Kingdom Central Council for Nursing, Midwifery and Health Visiting (UKCC), for example, revised its code in 1992 and it has been given extensive and sustained coverage in those professions. We asked a nurse in the oncology ward of a major teaching hospital whether the code was ever referred to in day-to-day practice. She replied to the effect that not only were copies displayed in prominent places but these were referred to on a regular basis. The code is referred to because the ethical component of their daily work is recognized as being extremely important.

I have not been able to identify any other environment in which a professional code is treated so seriously and visibly – except when things are going wrong. This is one of the major challenges for professional bodies which want to treat ethics seriously, and especially so in unregulated professions where members' careers are at little threat from such disciplinary processes as exist.

CONTENT OF THE CODES

The content of professional codes falls broadly into two categories: 'universal' themes, and 'stakeholder' themes.

POINTS TO PONDER

Do you work in a regulated profession, where breaking the ethical code could cause you to be banned from practising?

If so, how prominently displayed, and how often consulted and discussed, is your code of conduct? Could you immediately lay your hands on a copy? Can you remember its major demands?

If you are not in a regulated profession, what codes have you signed allegiance to? How seriously do you treat them?

If you are an official or an active senior member of an institute, ask yourself when last was the code of ethics given significant discussion time in the institute's topmost councils?

'Universal' Themes

These appear in the great majority of codes and are more or less independent of profession or industry. The five most frequent are as follows.

Professionalism

Virtually all codes call explicitly for the maintenance of high standards of 'professionalism' – and yet the term is rarely defined. It seems simply to be assumed that everyone knows what is meant. No doubt that is true in a very general sense, but most bodies would benefit from the kind of definition provided by the Institute of Management's Code of Conduct and Guides to Professional Practice (December 1993 edition):

> A professional man or woman is one who justifiably claims to provide an expert service of value to society, and who accepts the duties entailed by that claim, including:
>
> ■ the attainment and maintenance of high standards of education, training and practical judgement, and
>
> ■ honouring the special trust reposed by clients, employers, colleagues and the general public.

It goes on to describe ethical values which will characterize a true professional, 'among which a high place should be accorded to integrity, honesty, loyalty and fairness.'

Conflict of Interest

Some codes call explicitly for the declaration of such conflicts to all parties concerned; others give greater scope for handling them 'with integrity'. Avoiding the impairment of one's professional impartiality is the primary issue here. By and large the disclosure of an actual or potential conflict of interest is seen as adequate, rather than an insistence on withdrawal.

Maintaining Competence

Just over half of the professional bodies I have surveyed call explicitly for members to take positive steps to maintain their professional competence. I have been disappointed to discover

---

Your Own Institute – Some More Questions

Does your professional institute have a code of ethics? If so, how much emphasis is given to it?

Is it up to date? Does it explicitly cover the main ethical topics which you and your colleagues face in your work? Is it clearly worded? Does it recognize that dilemmas will arise, and give suggestions on how to approach them?

What is the process for keeping it up to date? Who is responsible for this process? Is that responsibility being discharged adequately?

Who is responsible for keeping the code before the minds of the membership?

---

that this is not more common, as in an age of rapid development in virtually every field of knowledge this matter of continual lifetime learning by professionals is critical. It is possible to consider that this is implied in the term 'professionalism', but I believe it to be of such importance as to warrant high-profile mention as a distinct and absolute professional responsibility.

Reputation of the Institute

Almost all professional institutes lay great stress on the reputation of the institute itself. Interestingly, at times I am almost led to believe that the emphasis is more on the reputation of the organization than on that of the profession which it represents, although many do use a form of words such as, 'The good standing of the institute and the profession.'

Bribery and Corruption

Most professional codes make specific mention of bribery. Questions of the permissibility of business gifts and hospitality are complex, and a variety of approaches is taken to the wording of these paragraphs. By and large, the professions seem to think in terms of (a) the consequences of a gift, ie, whether or not it leads to undue influence or unfair treatment, and (b) the intention of a gift, ie, whether or not it is designed to result in undue favour.

Interestingly, the Institute of Management's 1993 code and guidelines already referred to, in seeking to reflect the differing demands of different cultures and after unequivocally condemning bribery and corruption in an earlier section, appears to give a let-out by allowing behaviour, 'complying with established overseas customs and practices which are inconsistent in detail with the foregoing'. This is a complex issue which we can only flag up here without attempting to resolve it, but the words, 'in detail', added since the 1992 version, seem capable of very flexible interpretation.

'Stakeholder' Themes

The most commonly mentioned stakeholders in the codes which I have examined have been (i) the general public; (ii) clients; and (iii) employees, with suppliers and competitors mentioned by a few.

General Public

This is one of the most frequently mentioned stakeholder categories and it seems to be a catch-all heading. Most mentions of the general public are relatively vague, and it is not always clear in what ways their interests are supposed to be protected or how the professionals covered by the code might relate to them.

Clients

Protection and advancement of the client's interests are at the heart of many professional codes. Maintenance of an independent view has a high profile within this. The honesty of advertising is also important. None of the recent codes that I have seen bars professionals from advertising, but some lay down conditions. Many include an obligation to ensure that a member does not take on work for which he or she is not properly qualified and adequately experienced. A few prohibit certain methods of charging clients, such as banning 'payment by results', apparently on the basis that temptations to arrive at conclusions which benefit oneself or one's organization constitute a serious risk to professional impartiality and the priority of client interests.

Employees

Many codes encourage professionals to be active in developing the competence of their subordinate staff. In a few there is also the obligation to accept accountability for the actions of subordinates and for providing proper supervision. A small number refer specifically (although in widely differing words) to avoiding discrimination on grounds other than competence and performance, in particular race and sex.

Other Stakeholders

One notable stakeholder category – the natural environment – was very rarely referred to in the codes we examined in 1992, but since then there has been a trend for revisions to include it. In my own view codes should be worded so that not only is there a professional obligation to prevent as far as possible adverse impact upon the environment, but also wherever possible to seek to reverse damage already done. The Royal Society of Chemistry goes as far as this in an admirable passage:

> The activities of chemists can affect the environment. In the past these effects have often been detrimental, sometimes significantly and irreversibly so. The present day chemist has a moral as well as any legal duty to minimise and if possible reverse adverse effects on the environment.

Very few professional codes refer to other professions, or to members having to work in concert with or on behalf of members of other professions whose codes may impinge on the work in hand; nor do they recognize that members themselves may simultaneously be members of other professional bodies.

Employers are mentioned by several, especially with respect to conflicts of interest and confidentiality. One code in our sample specifically states that the public interest and the dignity of the profession come before responsibility to the employer, while another assures members of support in cases where public/ professional interest clashes with the wishes of an employer, implying support, in extremis, for 'whistleblowing'.

STYLE OF PROFESSIONAL CODES

Clarity

In the initial survey we applied a simple test of intelligibility by looking at each sentence and marking it in terms of its length and the simplicity of its construction. One scored 100 per cent, ie, every sentence was extremely clear. The worst scored 17 per cent, that is 83 per cent of the sentences were either very long or contorted in structure, or both. Some professional codes are so difficult to disentangle that I cannot imagine anyone ever reading them.

Style

Some codes read like detailed rule books, while others are statements of core values for the profession expressed in few words on one side of paper. The rule book approach covers more issues in precise terms, but it is by its nature less flexible, being more difficult to apply to situations which are not exactly as described in the text.

Another aspect of style is the degree to which the code is expressed in positive terms rather than as a series of prohibitions. By far the majority in my collection are phrased positively, encouraging desirable behaviours rather than condemning the undesirable, and this appears to me to be preferable although some prohibitions (such as those against bribery) certainly are necessary.

Presentation

Standards vary widely. Some documents are clearly developed with a view to being used; they are easy to follow, and printed in a form which is easy to read. Others are, to say the least, confused and confusing; it is difficult to imagine anyone attempting to read them unless it became unavoidable. In our survey one of the best in terms of clarity and structure of content was the most unattractively produced. Others are hidden away inside membership packs and lengthy constitutional documents, so that it takes a major search to find them.

SUMMARY AND PRACTICAL LESSONS

In keeping with the highly practical orientation of this book I will close this chapter with some action points for those concerned with developing or updating professional codes of conduct.

Be Clear about the Purpose of the Code

Is it being written simply because it is the done thing for a professional organization to have one? Is it primarily intended for practical guidance of members in day-to-day situations? Is it intended to be enforceable? Make certain that you know, and agree with all concerned, why you are developing the code. Clarity of purpose will greatly aid clarity of presentation.

Be Clear about the Formal Status of the Code

The intended status of the code therefore needs to be thought through carefully. Regulated professions, in which the institute in effect awards (and occasionally withdraws) a licence to practise, clearly need far more formal documents than those which are in a position to publish only guidance. In regulated professions the definition of (for example) such terms as, 'infamous conduct' and 'incompetence' are critical to the continued professional standing and livelihoods of members. Legal precision is essential and top quality advice should be sought in that respect – not, in my view, primarily to determine the content but rather to ensure that its phrasing is legally watertight. Associated disciplinary processes will need to be thought out, and also must be legally defensible.

At the other end of the spectrum there are institutes which are voluntary associations of professionals who can quite easily continue to practise without membership and in which the sanction of discipline is very weak. It may, in fact, be pointless to have a disciplinary process at all, or you may wish to have some process by which, in extremis, to expel members who are damaging the institute's or the profession's reputation even though such individuals will not as a consequence be prevented from practising. This matter needs to be thought through carefully at the very commencement of a code development exercise.

Decide on a Desirable Level of Detail

As indicated several times in this and previous chapters, a code may be developed at different levels. The following are the three main alternatives for a professional code: (1) a concise statement of core values or principles; (2) an extended code with items relating to the major ethical issues facing members; and (3) a detailed rule book. The middle level is most common. It should be possible to fit this onto one or two sides of paper in fairly large type. This middle level may call for additional practical guidelines to help members apply the principles to real life, but in our view level 3 is rarely appropriate.

If a rule book seems inevitable, for example in tightly regulated environments such as some healthcare professions, then a shorter values statement should also be produced. This should indicate the basis on which the edifice of rules is founded and enable people to develop approaches to situations which are not covered by any rule, or where apparent conflict between two or more rules has to be resolved. Generalized reference to 'professional values' does not help anyone greatly. However comforting it might be to think that everyone knows what 'professional values' are, one cannot assume this. They need to be spelled out and explained in simple terms (not philosophical argument) and with illustrations.

Decide on the Major Themes to be Covered

The topics covered should normally include those listed above as 'universal' themes plus others especially relevant to the particular profession or industry. Members may then find it helpful to have the main body structured around the most significant 'stakeholders' (clients, employees, suppliers, community, etc.) Alternatively, you might have the code itself as a short summary of principles, and then create supplements or explanatory notes to cover stakeholder relationships. The logic is very similar to that discussed in Chapter 9 in connection with company codes.

Ensure its Relevance to Members

Very few professional codes seem to take account of the variety of different types of employment in which members might be engaged. Some distinguish between self-employed professionals and those engaged as employees, and some recognize the particular situation of those working as independent consultants. Most, however, do not. Give careful attention to this point so that the document will be seen as relevant to professional life. A supplement containing guidance notes on its application within the different employment contexts might be considered.

DESIGN AND DEVELOPMENT PROCESS TO GAIN COMMITMENT

Finally, a professional body about to work on a new code should think through the process by which it is to be developed and agreed. To what extent will you consult with members about the issues which concern them? How will you ensure that the code is made relevant to as broad a spectrum of members as possible? How will you draw them into the actual work of development?

Some institutes will wish to use their geographic branch or chapter structures to stimulate debate. One association developed a draft in a small subcommittee of its elected council, and then invited all members to participate in discussion sessions at which first the general principles, and then the draft itself, were debated. This certainly led to a more balanced and comprehensive document, although the amount of effort was considerable. However you proceed, have in the front of your mind the need to avoid your professional code being seen as just another piece of administrative paperwork to file away.

18

Business Ethics and NGOs

Many managers, especially those in industrial organizations, may find it strange to read a suggestion that they
might benefit from the work of non-governmental
organizations, or NGOs – organizations of activist volunteers. They
are more accustomed to being on the opposite side of an
argument. Maybe their company has been condemned (in their
view misleadingly) for using material manufactured by children
working under little better than slave conditions in some obscure
Eastern country. Or possibly they've had a picket at the factory
gate declaring war on polluters in spite of the fact that only last
month they completed the installation of the most sophisticated
air-exhaust-cleaning process anywhere in the world in their
industry. Or maybe their product was featured in a recent
comparative study of safety features and condemned on the basis
of tests which, in their view, go far beyond the requirements of
any national or international standards and in any case are
technically flawed and meaningless.

WHAT ARE NGOs?

There are many kinds of NGO. Some are local; others national;
yet others are major international organizations with large
resources and decades of experience in their fields. Some
concentrate on a single issue. Others are more broadly based.
Some focus on the problems and sufferings of people, while others
work for lessening of human impact on the natural environment.
Some have no understanding of the business world and its
technologies (or indeed of their own dependence on it for their
way of life); others are not only knowledgeable but exist in order
to support and to strengthen business, even though in the process
they may wish to change it. Some, such as the International
Chamber of Commerce and the World Business Council for
Sustainable Development, are themselves organizations of
business people.

I am not at all certain that the negative term, 'non-governmental' is a useful one – except when such organizations are present at intergovernmental conferences and need to be distinguished from official national delegations. Outside of that context it would seem better to use a positive term such as 'voluntary organizations'. Many descriptions are applied to the current worldwide upsurge of voluntary organizations – terms such as Civil Society, the Third Sector, Grass-Roots Democracy – including charitable and philanthropic organizations, think tanks, pressure groups, all in the not-for-profit category. However, the term NGO is now in widespread use, more often as an acronym than in full, so I will continue to use it here for convenience.

Some exist to address very real and serious issues in society which are well-understood by the population as a whole, and therefore can draw on considerable public sympathy. Others, for one reason or another, have no media support for their cause; it is not fashionable. Yet others are 'on a loser' as minority movements with little or no chance of making any permanent impact – unless, of course, they are simply ahead of their times, and only the far future will tell.

Their level of professionalism varies considerably. Some employ leading international experts in their fields to research and communicate their case, so ensuring that they speak with authority. Some have, over a period of many years, come themselves to be leading authorities in their fields. Others, sadly, are amateurish in the worst sense of the word, grasping for any argument that seems to reinforce their case whether or not it can be justified logically or supported with evidence.

Points to Ponder

Which NGOs are engaged in work relevant to your industry, its suppliers and its customers?

What arrangements do you have in place for meaningful dialogue?

Are you active in business-sponsored NGOs in these same fields?

Ways of Working – With or Against Industry

There are NGOs whose mind-set is totally confrontational. Others, however, are keen to work alongside governmental and industrial bodies, even though they may dislike much about them, in order to encourage progress constructively down the road of change.

Some NGO criticism of industry, especially of multinational (or transnational) corporations, is extremely general in nature. Big business corporations are seen as inevitably, inherently evil. The alleged sins of one are presented as though they are typical of all. The mistakes and malpractices of transnational corporations are highlighted. Their many social programmes and positive contributions to the localities in which they operate are ignored, while any criticism by aggrieved individuals is easily assumed to be justified.

Other NGOs take a completely different approach. Transparency International, for example, has been mentioned several times in this book. Its dedication to the cause of eradicating corruption in international business transactions is undeniable. It recognizes, however, that campaigning on the basis of accusations against companies, governments and individuals involved in corruption will not be the most productive approach to making the necessary changes. Investigation of incidents is therefore not its style. Work toward the transformation of institutions, and the development of effective legislation and regulatory processes, is seen as best done without condemnation of people who have simply worked within the structures as they found them. Many other NGOs may consider this approach weak and over-tolerant of wrongdoing. The test will be the degree of change over coming years.

BUSINESS–NGO COOPERATION

A small number of NGOs are either candidly or in an underhand manner subversive. They exist to destroy, but not to build. Thankfully, few fall into this category. The great majority are composed of sincere, well-informed people concerned to become involved with the difficulties, the pains of this world. They are to be admired for their self-sacrificial efforts, and encouraged to think through their area of concern ever more comprehensively. Business and public organizations can help.

The building of a better society is in the interest of all. There is a school of business ethics thinking which I consider to be seriously unethical. It argues that for a company to devote resources to anything which does not contribute to its profit is theft from the shareholders. In its ultimate form this leads to a philosophy of zero community involvement at local, national and international level. It fails to recognize that many socially constructive initiatives which may not have a direct impact on the bottom line nevertheless do have a long-term benefit for everyone, including the company, for example by the development of a better educated, healthier workforce. It also fails to recognize that the company's privileges under law have been granted by society, and that legal privileges in society carry with them the moral obligations of citizenship.

Many of the objectives of NGOs, social and environmental, at home and overseas, coincide with the long-term interests of business. More cooperation could be mutually beneficial. One danger is that in some instances a proportion of activists may consider this to be collaborating with the enemy. It is very easy in a large business to find something that has gone wrong and to condemn, then to complain that it is impossible to cooperate with 'a company that behaves like this'. A certain generosity of spirit is necessary to work together in the understanding that all organizations of human beings are going to have flaws somewhere, and sometimes quite serious ones at that, but it is nevertheless worth working together toward something better.

It might seem rather strange to some to discover that a major motor manufacturer is a member of an environmentalist organization. The CERES organization (the Coalition for Environmentally Responsible Economies) developed what were initially known as the Valdez Principles in 1989 as a ten-point code for corporations which does not pretend that all the problems have been solved. CERES calls for people from different backgrounds and with different perspectives to work together to find ways forward, 'to transform an historically conflicting relationship into one of mutual respect and cooperation.'

Companies such as General Motors and the Polaroid Corporation are signatories to the CERES Principles in addition to more expected organizations such as Tom's of Maine and The Body Shop. Executives from companies like General Motors sit at the same table as environmentalists from organizations such as the Sierra Club searching together for shared perspectives and exploring the complexities of managerial decisions which will have environmental consequences. The box below gives the CERES Principles in full. This approach might to considerable advantage be emulated by companies and organizations in conflict over other, non-environmental, issues as well as being spread more widely outside the United States and what is at present a relatively small number of companies.

THE CERES PRINCIPLES

By adopting these Principles, we publicly affirm our belief that corporations have a responsibility for the environment, and must conduct all aspects of their business as responsible stewards of the environment in a manner that protects the Earth. We believe that corporations must not compromise the ability of future generations to sustain themselves.

We will update our practices constantly in light of advances in technology and new understandings in health and environmental science. In collaboration with CERES, we will promote a dynamic process to ensure that the Principles are interpreted in a way that accommodates changing technologies and environmental realities. We intend to make consistent, measurable progress in implementing these Principles and to apply them to all aspects of our operations throughout the world.

Protection of the biosphere
We will reduce and make continual progress towards eliminating the release of any substance that may cause environmental damage to the air, water, or the earth or its inhabitants. We will safeguard all habitats affected by our operations and will protect open spaces and wilderness, while preserving biodiversity.

Sustainable use of natural resources
We will make sustainable use of renewable natural resources, such as water, soils and forests. We will conserve non-renewable natural resources through efficient use and careful planning.

Reduction and disposal of wastes
We will reduce and where possible eliminate waste through source reduction and recycling. All waste will be handled and disposed of through safe and responsible methods.

Energy conservation

We will conserve energy and improve the energy efficiency of our internal operations and of the goods and services we sell. We will make every effort to use environmentally safe and sustainable energy sources.

Risk reduction

We will strive to minimize the environmental, health and safety risks to our employees and the communities in which we operate through safe technologies, facilities and operating procedures, and by being prepared for emergencies.

Safe products and services

We will reduce and where possible eliminate the use, manufacture or sale of products and services that cause environmental damage or health or safety hazards. We will inform our customers of the environmental impacts of our products or services and try to correct unsafe use.

Environmental restoration

We will promptly and responsibly correct conditions we have caused that endanger health, safety or the environment. To the extent feasible, we will redress injuries we have caused to persons or damage we have caused to the environment and will restore the environment.

Informing the public

We will inform in a timely manner everyone who may be affected by conditions caused by our company that might endanger health, safety or the environment. We will regularly seek advice and counsel through dialogue with persons in communities near our facilities. We will not take any action against employees for reporting dangerous incidents or conditions to management or to appropriate authorities.

Management commitment

We will implement these Principles and sustain a process that ensures that the Board of Directors and Chief Executive Officer are fully informed about pertinent environmental issues and are fully responsible for environmental policy. In selecting our Board of Directors, we will consider demonstrated environmental commitment as a factor.

Audits and reports

We will conduct an annual self-evaluation of our progress in implementing these Principles. We will support the timely creation of generally accepted environmental audit procedures. We will annually complete the CERES Report, which will be made available to the public.

Disclaimer

These Principles establish an environmental ethic with criteria by which investors and others can assess the environmental performance of companies. Companies that endorse these Principles pledge to go voluntarily beyond the requirements of the law. The terms 'may' and 'might' in Principles one and eight are not meant to encompass every imaginable consequence, no matter how remote. Rather, these Principles obligate endorsers to behave as prudent persons who are not governed by conflicting interests and who possess a strong commitment to environmental excellence and to human health and safety. These Principles are not intended to create new legal liabilities, expand existing rights or obligations, waive legal defences, or otherwise affect the legal position of any endorsing company and are not intended to be used against an endorser in any legal proceeding for any purpose.

(Quoted here in full by kind permission of CERES)

Working with the NGOs

Is there a better way to develop relationships with NGOs which are critical of one's company's activities? Surely there must be. Without for one minute suggesting that it will be possible to create a co-operative climate between every company and the more aggressive single-issue campaigners, the fact remains, as we have already seen, that many responsible groups are working together on matters of great importance to the future of commerce and industry.

Why not talk *with* some of the pressure groups? See whether, in fact, you have shared concerns. Make sure that the right people are doing the talking on your behalf. If, for example, you are discussing environmental impact reduction with an NGO which has named you as polluting a river in the Far East you probably have a senior person responsible for developing systems for environmental management (for example, to meet ISO 14000) who will bring more to the meeting than your corporate PR manager. You may need to keep a sharp eye out for hidden agendas, and for subversives, but most of the time you will be dealing with serious-minded people who might well be able to contribute something to your own organization's thinking. Why not explain some of the dilemmas you have faced in arriving at the way you currently do things? Many activists genuinely do not understand the complexity of management dilemmas; the conversation might well help them to develop a broader perspective. Many managers do not see the social and environmental impacts of their decisions; such exchanges might help the more open-minded individuals to do so.

You will need to sift out trivialities, genuine misunderstandings, passing fashions and minority fads, but you should also search out the underlying issues. There may be more there than you thought. There may be long-term issues which you had not considered when making that recent investment decision or carrying through that plant relocation. Think, on the other hand, of the potential impact on your corporate reputation if you constantly refuse to talk with leaders in the organizations of civil society.

The fortunes of many sustainable development, human rights and environmental protection NGOs were considerably advanced by their role in the UNCED conference in Rio de Janeiro in 1992. Not only did NGOs receive positive attention at this event but they were also able to meet and discuss together as never before with a view to the development of many joint strategies. Many smaller bodies came together to reinforce one another, agreed shared principles on which they would work, and articulated values and beliefs which, if implemented, must eventually change dramatically the conduct of the world economy.

Much of the talk and writing was idealistic, but countries and companies would be ill-advised to ignore this global movement. It may in parts be ill-informed. It may in parts be unrealistic in its aspirations. But equally companies may be closing their eyes to global inevitabilities. It surely would be better for the transnationals to start thinking and acting radically now, while the wilder dreams of single-issue campaigners are still capable of being moderated by a broader perspective, than to discover in ten years time that public opinion, stoked by sensational reporting, forces irrational business decisions. In any case, should not major corporations also be radical?

Investigators and Auditors

Mention has already been made of Transparency International's policy of not investigating specific instances of corruption, or of pursuing companies for their past behaviour. Greenpeace, on the other hand, in its environmental work, has a history of confronting governments and companies with which it disagrees, and its reputation in most of the business world is not high. Publication of volumes attacking business-linked environmental organizations under titles such as *Anti-Environmental Organizations* and *The Greenpeace Book of Greenwash* does little to foster future constructive relationships. In spite of this, however, it has in recent years been making some efforts in cooperating with businesses to find more environmentally friendly methods of working, and has started to publish practical solutions to some environmental problems.

An example of an organization which confronted many British companies, but in a responsible manner, in the early 1990s is New Consumer. Its report, *Changing Corporate Values*, was published in 1992 with the subtitle, 'A guide to social and environmental policy and practice in Britain's top companies'. One hundred and twenty-eight companies, accounting for 35–40 per cent of UK consumer spending in 1989, were assessed according to criteria ranging from their treatment of women and ethnic minorities to their environmental impact and level of military sales. To a significant degree their catalogue of issues reflects the then-fashionable concerns at the radical end of the political spectrum. Having said that, most ethical issues at the core of the policy making and daily operation of businesses are hidden from view and are not susceptible to assessment from outside. It is arguable that they measured what they could. The survey was carried out largely by asking the companies to complete a questionnaire. Some did so comprehensively; others refused totally.

The fact that a significant number of companies declined to co-operate with a survey which was being conducted in a responsible manner suggests that not only some NGOs but also many business organizations think in confrontational terms. Could it be that some companies were afraid of what the survey might have shown?

THE NGOs THEMSELVES

Meanwhile there are questions to ask about the conduct of NGOs themselves. Like any other organization an NGO needs to carry out its multiple-level stakeholder analysis as described in Chapter 5. Its ethical imperatives extend not only to its campaigning subject matter but to all aspects of its operation. NGOs are values-driven organizations. In that sense they are different from the majority of businesses, and in a sense like religious organizations which often have similar problems of poor management. All too often the existence of a strong values base deceives people into thinking that other vital aspects of professional management, such as planning systematically and strategically, and leading people effectively, can be neglected. The management of people, who are assumed to be self-motivated, is a common gap. A recent paper by Rebecca Macnair highlights the complexities of managing in this environment and many of the shortcomings.

Codes of conduct for such organizations should have a great deal in common with those for other kinds of organization. Differences will arise from NGOs' involvement in campaigning, in fund-raising, and in their specific areas of specialism but all sectors have, for example, suppliers and staff. As to campaigning, Des Wilson's book, *Campaigning: The A–Z of Public Advocacy*, contains ten Principles in its opening chapter. Of the first four three are clearly ethical: the first is, 'Tell the truth'; the third, 'Maintain a sense of perspective', and the fourth, 'Abhor violence'. As to fund-raising, absolute transparency is vital; there must be total honesty with contributors so that none gives to a cause with which they do not sympathize.

The Ethical NGO

While campaigning against the immorality of business, how much thought do you give to your own conduct?

How ethically robust are your employment policies?

How honest is your advertising and publicity?

Do you acknowledge improvements that have been made?

Do you use exaggeration either in campaigning or fund-raising?

Of codes concentrating on principles of operational conduct an excellent example is that of the International Red Cross and Red Crescent movement. After delineating the principles on which disaster relief is carried out (with a short paragraph to expand on each of ten statements) it goes on to identify other agencies influencing the environment within which their work is carried out. The implications of the code for each of them are spelled out, with recommendations to governments of disaster-affected areas, to governments of donor countries, and to intergovernmental organizations.

BUSINESS AND NGOs – WHERE FROM HERE?

As anyone reading the above paragraphs will be aware there is no question of NGOs being perfect. They have many flaws, and a very few may even be dangerous. But they are not all the same. They will not go away. There is a strong sense of disenchantment with conventional political processes, especially among the young. A new 'grass-roots democracy' is taking shape in the form of a multiplicity of organizations of civil society loosely networked together. They may not always be led or run from the true grass-roots; they may not always show many of the characteristics of democracy; but governments and business cannot afford to ignore them.

Businesses can expect to hear much from NGOs in the future. Much of what they hear will not be palatable. Some of it will be, to speak frankly, idealistic, narrow-minded nonsense. But it will not all be like that. Much of the comment will flow from extensive serious research, and will have identified serious problems. Businesses, and governments, need to learn to listen. There is much talk in the field of organizational development these days about the 'learning organization'. The idea is that organizations as well as individuals need to learn continually, and to be prepared then to internalize that learning, sometimes by small-scale incremental change, sometimes by major shifts of policy and practice. It has been my belief for many years that in order to have a true learning organization one must first build a 'listening organization'. One of the early questions in designing the listening process must be, 'To whom and to what do we need to listen?'

Responsible NGOs are owed attention by the business world. They will often provide advance warning of what could eventually become deadly serious developments in the global economy.

Question to companies building 'a learning organization'

To learn we must listen

Are you prepared to listen thoughtfully to voluntary organizations in civil society, even to those whose campaigning style you dislike?

Companies cannot afford to close their ears. In 1993 a toy factory in Thailand burned down; 188 people were killed and 469 injured. Why? Because there were no sprinklers, no alarms, and blocked fire exits. The factory collapsed within 15 minutes. What is the Western toy industry doing about this kind of situation? What are other industries doing which take advantage of minimal safety and other humane regulations elsewhere in the world in order to produce cheaply? The World Development Movement (which was also actively involved in the Pergau Dam affair) has publicized this Thai incident in the West. At present it is a small voice. But once morally aware consumers (and there is an increasing proportion of such throughout the developed world) become aware of these matters market shares could be lost and profits collapse – and for what? For a proud unwillingness to listen!

Useful References

Richard Adams, Jane Caruthers and Sean Hamil (1991) *Changing Corporate Values*, Kogan Page, London.

Rebecca Macnair (1996) *Room for Improvement: The management and support of relief and development workers*, ODI, London.

Des Wilson (1993) *Campaigning: The A–Z of Public Advocacy*, Hawksmere, London.

19

Business Ethics and Faith

To the west of Chicago you will find a rapidly expanding sprawl of modern towns, many of which contain the headquarters buildings of business corporations. As you walk into the front entrance hall of one of these you might notice a marked contrast within the design of the building. Whereas almost everything else in the building is constructed so that it can be changed easily, to adapt to the constantly changing needs of the business, one thing stands solid and stable, deliberately distinct from all around it – a wall of stone.

On this wall are inscribed the four principles by which this organization aspires to conduct its affairs, listed as objectives: to grow profitably, to pursue excellence, and to help people develop. But I've listed them in reverse order. The first, standing out at the head of the list reads: 'To honor God in all we do'.

Of course, you might well think, we're close to the town of Wheaton, a focal point of conservative evangelical theology and evangelism, with Bible-believing college and mission headquarters almost on every street corner This must be some missionary enterprise.

No, this is not a church, and not a mission; nor is it the HQ block of a charitable foundation. It is a business, and no ordinary business at that. This is a Fortune 500 company which has delivered increased revenues and profits consistently, year after year, for more than a quarter of a century. This is an organization used as a case study at the Harvard Business School. It is a company which employs and manages over 200,000 people around the world with revenues over $4 billion per annum. The Servicemaster Company (providing cleaning and maintenance services around the globe) was founded by people with strong faith, and has seen no reason over the years to move from that initial primary driver: we seek to honor God in all we do.

As current Chairman Bill Pollard says, this is not an excluding statement, making life difficult for staff who do not share the faith of the founders. 'Rather it is the most *including* statement we could make. It leads us to treat every man or woman, employee or customer, as an individual of profound personal worth, made by God in the image of God.'

CHRISTIAN CHURCHES AND THE BUSINESS WORLD

The involvement of churches and their leaders in economic and industrial affairs has had a chequered history. In the United States this has had much to do with the 'privatization' of religion. Despite the example of Servicemaster quoted above, there is a widely held view (though more common among the intellectual and artistic elites than the people as a whole) that religion belongs behind the closed doors of the private home and within the walls of church buildings but certainly not in the public square, the marketplace or the workplace. In the UK, while there has been a certain amount of this kind of thinking, probably more significant has been the tendency to view 'men of the cloth' as ill-informed and naive with regard to economic matters – sometimes, sadly, a valid comment. Hearing clerics pronouncing against 'private profit' as though it were a dirty, immoral concept does nothing to endear them to the hearts of company leaders.

The situation is now changing. In the United States, more than 85 per cent of the population describe themselves as Christian and more than 50 per cent actually attend church. In the UK the first figure is a little under 70 per cent (although church attendance is lower at around 11 per cent, varying widely between areas of the country) and in both countries there is increasingly a tendency to ask: 'What implications should my faith have for how I behave from Monday to Friday, not only at home and among my friends but also in my place of work? How can I continue living a fragmented life, in which I have high standards of honesty and integrity in relationships with family and friends but allow them to be diluted as soon as I reach the office?'

In England, at one Church of England theological college (Ridley Hall, Cambridge) its then Principal (Hugo de Waal, now Bishop of Thetford) some years ago commenced 'The God on Monday Project', designed to study the implications of faith for business life. A programme of research, teaching, writing and public seminars continues, including provision of teaching for future Anglican clergy about the ethical dimensions of working life. Now going under the name, 'Faith in Business', seminar leaders include not only college staff but also senior people from the worlds of commerce, industry and the professions who have themselves wrestled from a Christian perspective with dilemmas in practical business life.

On both sides of the Atlantic many of the leading academic centres in the field of business ethics have church connections. The business ethics chair at the London Business School is currently occupied by a Jesuit priest, and this is far from unusual in the United States.

A small Protestant denomination, the Mennonite movement (named after one of its early Dutch leaders) has from its very beginnings in 16th century central Europe emphasized the practical living-out of Christian belief, combined with a strong sense of community. As with other faith communities, conflicts between community norms and entrepreneurial style have not always been easy to handle. Today, however, their organization, Mennonite Economic Development Associates (MEDA), flourishes in many parts of the world, from Moscow to Mexico, exploring ways of integrating faith and work. Their bimonthly magazine, *The Marketplace*, which has run successfully now for over 25 years, declares its purposes as: (i) to help business people apply Christian faith to the world of work, and (ii) to provide a forum to examine business ethics, workplace relationships, lifestyle and public responsibility from a Christian perspective.

MEDA's 1995 annual four-day convention in Pennsylvania attracted over 500 people to ponder the theme, 'Just rewards: who benefits from your business?' The convention had a cast of speakers (both from Mennonite churches and other Christian traditions) which included not only pastors and theologians, but also leaders of businesses from the small and regional to international corporations, combining constructively the input of economics and theology from academic speakers with the feet-on-the-ground experience of people actually running organizations.

THE ROMAN CATHOLIC CONTRIBUTION

Since the late 19th century there has developed a strong tradition of profound thought on economic issues within the Catholic Church. Many leading academic business ethicists are Catholic priests.

It started effectively in May 1891 with an encyclical letter, *Rerum Novarum*, from the then Pope (Leo XIII) which explored especially the relationships between the state, employers and the workers. It called on legal authorities to 'remove early the causes from which it would seem that conflict between employers and workers is bound to arise', and continued, 'No one may with impunity outrage the dignity of man, which God Himself treats with great reverence.' Clearly denying the widespread traditional view that the Church is on the side of the rich and powerful he called for 'Oppressed workers... to be liberated from the savagery of greedy men.' He explored the concept of the 'Just wage' and appealed for employers to desist from over-pressurizing the workforce.

Down the years there has followed a succession of papal encyclicals dealing with social and employment matters. Pius XI issued *Quadragessimo Anno* in 1931, and John XXIII, *Mater et Magistra* in 1961. Most recently on the centenary of *Rerum Novarum* came another encyclical, this time from John Paul II: *Centessimus Annus*. The social teaching of the Church has developed through this time, addressing new circumstances and conditions of society as they have emerged.

In the business world the International Christian Union of Business Executives (UNIAPAC), although officially now ecumenical, is in most countries largely a Catholic organization devoted to promulgating the Church's social teachings. It operates at several levels, from groups which focus on individual young executives and their families to international conferences in which bishops and top corporate executives can think together over current major issues such as unemployment.

ORTHODOX BUSINESS THINKING

For the past several generations the majority of the Christian world represented by the Orthodox tradition (countries such as Bulgaria, Romania, Russia, Serbia and the Ukraine) have been controlled by proponents of the communist ideology. Understandably little thinking about economic life as it is known in the West has emerged from the Orthodox churches. This is now beginning to change, although inevitably the process of adjustment to forms of market economics will take some years. Postcommunist economies will hopefully mature into forms which are suitable for their situation, rather than slavishly copying the West with all its failings. It is also to be hoped that in the course of the transition these countries, and we in the West also, will be given the benefits of profound Orthodox consideration of the world of work and enterprise. The Keston College Journal, *Religion and Society*, published an interesting paper in 1995 entitled: 'Old belief and work', in which Mikhail Roschin discussed the role of the 'Old believers' movement within the Russian Orthodox Church in the economic development of Russia before the revolution. He points out that almost two-thirds of the trading class in Russia were old believers. This could be a fascinating avenue for further research into whether there was something approximating to a Protestant work ethic in this section of the Russian church.

CORE PRINCIPLES OF BUSINESS INTEGRITY

In Chapter 4 we looked at the subject of shared values, and then in Chapter 9 took this a step further into the development of corporate codes of ethics. At the time I asked the question, 'Will any set of values suffice'. There is a tendency for many people in the modern world to claim that everyone has their own values, and no one can claim that theirs are better than anyone else's. I answered that in Chapter 4 by arguing that capitalist market economics can only survive if it maintains the foundation of moral values on which it was originally constructed. If capitalism allows its prosperity to fuel yet more and more materialistic self-centredness, forgetting the essentials of trust, integrity and justice it will collapse under its own weight like a house built on sand. Marx was wrong about many things, but history may yet prove him right in claiming, 'What the bourgeoisie produces above all is its own gravediggers.'

In developing statements of corporate values and codes of ethics there will, and should, be considerable differences between organizations in how they are expressed and made relevant to their situations. If, however, a code does not contain at its heart such basics of moral integrity as honesty, justice, and respect and concern for others, it would be better not written – that is, unless the board has decided to come clean, to scrap the hypocrisy, and to declare clearly to the world: 'We have no principles beyond complying with the law where we think we might get caught if we don't; apart from that it is every man for himself and the survival of the fittest.'

Two or three years ago I was involved in an extended exercise in post-communist Central Europe with business people, ethicists and theologians from both sides of the former divide, examining principles of business conduct in that difficult environment. After many months of discussions I attempted to distil out of all the notes some answers to the question: what are the Christian principles of behaviour which are most relevant to the world of work?

First, it is important to recognize a strong Biblical orientation in favour of work and business. Work is seen as a constructive thing; human creativity is viewed as reflecting the image of a creative God. Work was an important theme in the post-Reformation period as there developed what eventually became known as the Protestant work ethic, too often today confused with a kind of workaholism. Dedication, honesty and integrity are everywhere emphasized, and justice is a strong theme in both Old and New Testaments.

We looked at the various descriptions of good behaviour given in the New Testament – by Jesus (eg, the Sermon on the Mount), by Paul ('The fruit of the Spirit' and 'The new man'), by Peter ('virtue' and the 'divine nature'), and by James ('The wisdom from above').

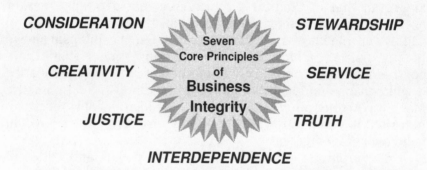

Figure 19.1 *Seven core principles of business integrity*

The seven core principles shown in Figure 19.1, while reflecting biblical Christian thought, are expressed in modem language such as might be used in an ordinary business environment. It is important to make them easily accessible by people who do not share the same faith.

They do not pretend to cover every aspect of business life; and they allow certain assumptions such as that wealth-creation, efficiency, effectiveness and economy, along with the acceptance and reward of risk are valid – but not to the exclusion of every other consideration, and not without self-control and a balanced perspective on the benefits and dangers of material prosperity.

The seven principles are expressions of a desire for human dignity and wholeness in the workplace. Their thoughtful application should humanise the otherwise mechanical processes of wealth-creation and efficiency.

- *Stewardship* – none of our 'possessions' is ours for long; we will eventually leave them behind; we only have this earth's resources in our temporary care; do we treat them as ours to rape and to destroy at will? What will we leave for our successors, and for future generations?

- *Service* – true leadership is a service; in our organizations, how helpfully do we serve colleagues? How effectively do we serve our customers? How well do we serve our 'subordinates' by providing them with the setting in which to use their abilities?

- *Truth* – the ability to trust others to keep their word, and to honour their signatures to the very best of their abilities, is at the heart of economic life; how factual are our tax returns? How truthful is our advertising? and can the promises of sales people be relied upon? Truth is a universal requirement.

- *Interdependence* – do we recognize that a business organization (or organism) is like a body with interdependent parts? do we remember to provide reliable, high-quality service to our internal 'customers' – the colleagues who depend on us in order to perform their roles well?

- *Justice* – fairness in dealing with all those affected by the conduct of a business is vital if society is in the long-term to continue to renew its 'licence to operate'. How fair are our employment practices? How fair is our reward of performance? What justice do we allow to weaker parties in a negotiation?

- *Creativity* – the potential for human creativity in developing sound, profitable businesses is enormous; to what degree do our organizations give scope for this to be used? Do we still apply outmoded styles of management which stifle initiative, insisting on blind obedience?

- *Consideration* – to what degree do we give consideration to the interests an concerns of others? Have we allowed self-interest to become twisted, distorted into selfishness? Do we take account of the full range of people with a 'stake' in the behaviour of the organization? Who are our 'neighbours'?

OTHER WORLD FAITHS

I am better qualified to write from a Christian perspective, but I do recognize other faith communities are also actively involved in the debate about standards in business life. I am indebted to Simon Webley for the content of the following paragraph on Islamic business thinking. The Muslim world has long given considerable thought to how it can interface with a world economic system which is based strongly on the principle of earning and paying interest, which Islam forbids. Islamic banks have had to develop methods of operating effectively in the international sphere while maintaining their integrity.

Like Christianity and Judaism, Islam is a religion of a book, and the book deals with the practicalities of everyday life – not only formal acts of worship. The Koran gives instruction on justice (Maida, v.9): 'Stand out firmly for God, as witnesses to fair dealing.' It also recognizes that material goods are entrusted to us by God as His stewards (Sura 57 [iron] v 7): 'Spend of that whereof He has made you trustees'. The prophet Mohammed taught that no man will be allowed to proceed to his reward on the day of judgement until he has accounted for how he obtained his wealth and how he used it.

Jewish business ethics are being given a boost in the UK by the Jewish Association for Business Ethics. For Yom Kippur in 1995 they published a four-page folder to be used in synagogues, developed by the director of the Centre for Business Ethics at the Jerusalem College of Technology. For 24 days the confession 'We have done wrong' was repeated – ranging, on different days, from misuse of pension fund moneys to shoddy workmanship, and from tax evasion to obsession with career at the expense of family, community and God. Humiliating colleagues in front of others and exploiting other people's lack of knowledge were other themes highlighted to trigger confession, bringing the concept of sin and repentance right down to earth in terms of 9 to 5, Monday to Friday.

AN INTERFAITH BUSINESS CODE

The major faiths of the world are usually seen as mutually exclusive, and certainly with respect to their theologies that is true. However, in many areas of morality there are strongly shared ideals. On all sides it is admitted that believers, including leaders, do not always live up to these. Such failure, though, cannot excuse us from having the ideals before us, even if their primary role is to show us up for what we truly are.

'So what can we all, with our different religious backgrounds, agree on as basic standards in business life?' It was with this question in mind that HRH the Duke of Edinburgh, HRH the Crown Prince of Jordan and Sir Evelyn de Rothschild called together a group of senior representatives (industrialists, bankers, academics and clerics) of Islam, Judaism and Christianity. Meeting on a number of occasions over almost five years they eventually arrived at, and in 1994 published, 'An Interfaith Declaration: A Code of Ethics on International Business for Christians, Muslims and Jews'.

Simon Webley, who put together the final document, has in several places written and spoken of the process by which it was produced, and most recently (in an as yet unpublished paper presented to the July 1996 conference of the International Society for Business, Economics and Ethics in Tokyo) has discussed the four core values underlying the code:

> *Justice*
> *Mutual respect*
> *Stewardship*
> *Honesty*

Under the three headings of Business and Political Economy, The Policies of a Business, and Conduct of Individuals at Work, they provide guidelines consistent with the moral principles of the three major monotheistic faiths.

The greatest amount of detail is given in the second level, The Policies of a Business (see below). Although based on careful consideration of theological and moral issues – and in his Tokyo paper Simon Webley makes extensive reference to both the Bible and the Koran – the guidelines themselves deal in business language with practical matters as statements of best practice, structured around six stakeholder relationships.

Having come so far with the three major monotheistic faiths the next challenge must be for others to explore the degree to which a practical workable code of conduct can be developed to take account also of Eastern thought patterns flowing from Buddhism and Confucianism, from Hinduism and the Japanese Shinto religion.

Extract from

'An Interfaith Declaration: A Code of Ethics on International Business for Christians, Muslims and Jews'

a) *Employees*
Employees make a unique contribution to an organization; it follows that in their policies, businesses shall where appropriate, take notice of trade union positions and provide:
(i)   Working conditions that are safe and healthy and conducive to high standards of work.
(ii) Levels of remuneration that are fair and just, that recognise the employees' contribution to the organization and the performance of the sector of the business in which they work.
(iii) A respect for the individual (whether male or female) in their beliefs, their family responsibility and their need to grow as human beings. It will provide equal opportunities in training and promotion for all members of the organization. It will not discriminate in its policies on grounds of race, colour, creed, or gender.

b) *Providers of Finance*
A business cannot operate without finance. There is therefore, a partnership between the provider and the user. The company borrowing money shall give to the lender:
(i)   What has been agreed to be repaid at the due dates.
(ii) Adequate safeguards in using the resources entrusted.
(iii) Regular information on the operations of the business and opportunities to raise with directors matters concerning their performance.

c) *Customers*
Without customers a business cannot survive. In selling products or services, a company shall provide for the customer:
(i)   The quality and standard of service which has been agreed.

(ii)   After-sales service commensurate with the type of product or service and the price paid.

(iii) Where applicable, a contract written in unambiguous terms.

(iv)   Informative and accurate information regarding the use of the product or service especially where misuse can be dangerous.

d) *Suppliers*

Suppliers provide a daily flow of raw materials, products and services to enable a business to operate. The relationship with suppliers is normally a long term one and must therefore be based on mutual trust. The company shall:

(i)   Undertake to pay its suppliers promptly and in accordance with agreed terms of trade.

(ii) Not use its buying power in an unscrupulous fashion.

(iii) Require buyers to report offers of gifts or favours of unusual size or questionable purpose.

e) *Community (Local and National Government)*

While companies have an obligation to work within the law, they must also take into account the effects of their activities on local and national communities. In particular they shall:

(i)   Ensure that they protect the local environment from harmful emissions from manufacturing plant, excessive noise and any practice likely to endanger humans, animals or plant life.

(ii) Consider the social consequences of company decisions e.g. plant closures, choice of new sites or expansion of existing ones.

(iii) Not tolerate any form of bribery, extortion or other corrupt or corrupting practices in business dealings.

f) *Owners (shareholders)*

The shareholders undertake the risks of ownership. The elected directors shall:

i)   Protect the interests of shareholders.

ii)   See that the company's accounting statements are true and timely.

iii) See that shareholders are kept informed of all major happenings affecting the company.

By permission: The Calamus Foundation

MEETING A NEED

What can churches, or gatherings of people of other faiths, do to help people apply their moral principles to working life? Many people especially those who rarely enter one, think of churches as dark places in which ancient, obscure and nowadays irrelevant rituals are performed on a Sunday morning using unintelligible language, observed by congregations of elderly ladies. Most are very far from that, and exciting things are now happening.

In early 1996, to take just one example, I was invited to lead a full-day workshop on Christianity and business for a church in Paris. Around 25 men and women, mostly professional people aged between 30 and 40, spent the major part of a sunny Saturday in Spring in a light and airy church hall studying and discussing together a number of themes that they themselves had selected. This is not now particularly unusual, although it would have been so as recently as five years ago; and this is only one of the approaches that churches are adopting.

More and more clergy and other church leaders are now entering their ministries in mid-life having acquired experience of life in commerce and industry, which to most of their predecessors was a total mystery. What is more, many of these new leaders are not escapees from an industrial system in which they have been unsuccessful. Rather, having been successful in one environment they have felt a 'calling' to another.

This means that fewer pronouncements should in future be made on the ethics of business by religious leaders almost totally ignorant of the environment on which they are commenting. It means that more church leaders are likely to recognize the great gap in pastoral support and care which has existed in the past. It has been easy to recognize the pastoral needs of those recently 'made cruelly redundant by uncaring managers'. It has been far less easy for pastors to detect the cruel pressures of dilemma in the lives of those managers – who themselves are no longer sure of their career futures. More effort needs to be channelled into serving the pastoral needs of the apparently successful.

Islands of Integrity

Finally, on an encouraging note, in Romania in recent years I have been greatly impressed by a group of almost 50 small-scale entrepreneurs who, with the joint support of a local Catholic priest and a visiting Protestant missionary, meet together regularly to share experiences, to study, and to reinforce one another in an ambition to be 'Islands of integrity in a sea of corruption.' In a difficult situation they set an example for those of us living and working in easier environments.

Useful References

Richard Chewning (1984) (ed.) *Biblical Principles and Business – The Foundations*, Navpress, Colorado Springs.

Richard Chewning (1990) *Biblical Principles and Business – The Practice*, NavPress, Colorado Springs.

Max De Pree (1989) *Leadership is an Art*, Arrow, London.

Richard Harries (Bishop of Oxford) (1992) *Is there a Gospel for the Rich? The Christian in a Capitalist World*, Mowbray, London.

Richard Higginson (1993) *Called to Account*, Eagle, Guildford.

Leland Ryken (1990) *Work & Leisure in Christian Perspective*, Inter-Varsity Press, Leicester.

20

Academic Business Ethics

A significant academic phenomenon of recent years has been the birth of ethics research groups, ethics institutes, and ethics centres in colleges and universities around the world. Many of these focus on a theme such as 'business' or 'professional' ethics. Here is yet another indication of a widespread feeling, not restricted to any one geographical, cultural or religious setting, that something is wrong with the way people behave in this world, and that it needs to be investigated.

BUSINESS ETHICS TEACHING

I used the word 'investigated' carefully in the above paragraph. Unlike people in previous chapters who feel an obligation to persuade, and to make a difference in the world, many (perhaps most) academics involved in business ethics prefer to maintain something of a detachment from practice. They see their role as to think through issues, and to teach their students to analyse. They do not consider that education has as one of its objectives to guide the future behaviour of students.

This approach, of course, has its advantages and disadvantages. It avoids the danger of being accused of indoctrination rather than education. However, except in the hands of teachers with a rare combination of both intellectual and communication skills, it can also lead to a bland 'Your view is as valid as anyone else's' kind of relativism which fails to challenge. Maybe this is why so many ethics classes are thought of as make-weights in the curriculum. Just like religious education in schools, taught by teachers who don't believe their subject matter, and like sermons from pulpits where the preachers have long ago ceased to believe the truth of their message, they carry little force. Is this what young students, or older ones for that matter, want as preparation for a world which they know to be in a mess?

This is not to argue that professors should be forcing their own conclusions down the throats of their long-suffering students.

They should, however, be helping them to arrive at conclusions, and to think through the practical implications of these in a challenging manner.

In Chapter 19 we saw that, throughout a large proportion of the world, although there are differences in the acknowledged sources of moral and religious authority, there are many shared principles of good behaviour. The argument that values cannot be taught because everyone has their own, is fallacious. One aim of a good teacher must be to equip students to identify and to articulate their values as individuals, to understand the degree to which basic values such as truth, responsibility and humanity are shared with others around them, and to understand also the degree to which, and why, they differ in some areas from those of others.

Given that people have to live in this world not as isolated individuals but in communities, they need to be taught how to develop a body of shared values that can shape and inform the goals, style and decision making of an organization. They must be taught how to apply these to the issues of everyday business and professional life, and how to understand why others are behaving differently from what they would expect. They must be provided with skills in analysing and resolving dilemmas.

In order to comply with traditional academic criteria, no doubt it is necessary to study the thinkers of the past, and indeed it would be seriously remiss of any course designer to omit this. If, however, the output of a course is a group of well-read people who can only 'talk ethics' in jargon terms of Kantian this and Rawlsian that, then the business and professional world will not have been well-served.

Managerial and professional leaders of the future will need to understand how to integrate moral reasoning into business decision making (about, say, the most appropriate location for a new manufacturing plant for a toxic chemical, or whether to adopt a new way of showing a profit figure which is legally permissible but which may mislead) and to do so in a management committee room where no one else has ever heard of deontology or consequentialism.

This is a major challenge for the ethics institutes. I believe it to be a sound reason for rarely having a business or professional ethics unit within a philosophy department. There are, no doubt, some good ones; and yes, the input of philosophers is needed, but the aim must not be to convert managers and professionals into philosophers. It must be to provide practical skills of moral reasoning, indeed to incorporate these into the teaching of every professional topic.

A few years ago, when examining the moral dilemmas faced by managers in healthcare, I talked with several people involved in the teaching of medical ethics. Some medical schools scarcely seemed to cover the topic at all. Others had quite comprehensive modules which were treated seriously. The one which really impressed me, however, had only a short specialist course – but it then ensured that ethical considerations were explored in depth within each of the medical and surgical specialisms. Ethics was brought into touch with practical reality.

ETHICS CONFERENCES

I would not like the above to be interpreted as an attack on ethics teachers. There are some for whom I have the highest regard, although they may not agree with the above arguments. I have attended many academic conferences on business ethics in many countries. However, apart from the excellent series of one-day events held in recent years at the London Business School, relatively few have been a good use of time, apart from the discussions out of session and the relationships formed and sustained. Why? Because so many of the papers show little connection to the lives of real people practising management. Because so many of the presenters appear never to have worked in a business or other organizational environment outside of academia, and their perspectives are distorted by caricature. Because papers all too often are couched in jargonistic terms calculated to impress examiners or journal referees, rather than to speak to the needs of the practitioner. Because the conferences are usually academics talking to academics, with scarcely a handful of practitioners present to inject something of the real world, and to communicate the burning priorities or the broader perspectives of the business community.

Why, then, do I go to them? Because it is important to broaden one's vision, to see things from completely different points of view. Conferences give opportunities to discuss matters with highly intelligent and articulate people who come from totally different backgrounds from oneself. Also, having said all that, I believe that things are improving. Some conferences deliver good value. In the year that this book is being completed (1996) two outstanding programmes come to mind, both intended to bring together academic and business thinkers and practitioners on an international basis – organized respectively by the European Business Ethics Network (to be held in Germany) and the International Society for Business, Economics and Ethics (held in Japan).

ACADEMIA AND THE INTERNET

Possibly the most significant explosion in academic communication since the invention of the printing press is the World Wide Web. The two conferences mentioned above both publicized their programmes via Web pages and, in fact, the ISBEE conference made its papers available on the Web several weeks in advance of the conference, so that people who could not travel to Japan for the meetings were able to discuss points with the authors – even before the conference had taken place.

Several excellent resources on business ethics are now available from academic institutions around the world. Addresses for a selection of 'author's favourites' are given below. Some are valuable for the information they themselves contain (such as the calendar of events at the DePaul, Chicago Web site), while others provide extensive links onwards and outwards to a wide variety of other resources. In the early stages the World Wide Web consisted mostly of addresses which then passed one on to yet other addresses without ever delivering anything of very great substance. This has now changed. More and more valuable news reports, conference announcements and papers, research working papers, annual reports and magazine-style articles are emerging into general public view via this easy-to-access medium.

Of course, it can be time-consuming to track down what one is looking for, but the increasing power of the freely-available 'search engines' (such as Digital's Alta Vista – accessible at the URL address, http://www.altavista.digital.com/) is making this task much easier. It is also true that the Web, like a highway built with too few lanes to cope with the traffic flow, gets extremely congested and slows down at certain times of the day. In the UK, for example, it is best to rise early like the bird looking for its worm, approximately 5.00am to 7.00am being the most efficient time. This, however, is improving as additional equipment is installed around the world

The DePaul University Web pages include another innovation – an ethics journal in electronic format, the address for which is

Conference Announcements and Papers on the Web

European Business Ethics Network:
http://www.nijenrode.nl/research/eibe/eben/index.html

ISBEE World Congress – Japan 1996:
http://www.nd.edu:80/~isbee/papers.htm

Business Ethics Institutes, etc., on the Web

DePaul University – Chicago:
http://www.depaul.edu/ethics

Business Ethics Teaching Society:
http://www.usi.edu/bets/

European Business Ethics Network:
http://www.nijenrode.nl/research/eibe/eben/index.html

European Institute for Business Ethics, Nijenrode:
http://www.nijenrode.nl/research/eibe.html

International Society of Business, Economics and Ethics:
http://www.nd.edu:80/~isbee/

Applied Ethics Web Site:
http://www.ethics.ubc.ca/papers/wsotw.html

Directory of Business Ethics Institutes:
http://condor.depaul.edu/ethics/ethi1.html

Ethical Business (UK):
http://www.arq.co.uk/ethicalbusiness/index.htm

INDEX to ethical organizations etc., UK academic:
http://www.bath.ac.uk/Centres/Ethical/directry.htm

ISBEE List of Useful Web sites:
http://www.nd.edu:80/~isbee/links.htm

DePaul – Institute Newsletter:
http://condor.depaul.edu/ethics/newstop.html

On-Line of Journal of Ethics:
http://condor.depaul.edu/ethics/ethg1.html

included in the list. This promises to be an excellent addition to sources of high grade, thought-provoking papers to add to the conventional paper-based journals such as the *Journal of Business Ethics* (Canadian in editorial origin), the *Business Ethics: European Review* (based in the London Business School) and, commencing in 1997, a new Canadian-based journal, *Teaching Business Ethics*.

21

Business Ethics into the 21st Century

I n the 1960s and 1970s there was an upsurge of interest and activity in the general area of business ethics, especially in the United States, around the theme of 'corporate social responsibility'. Then came the 1980s and their focus on self-interest. The battle to improve behaviour in the business world seemed to be lost.

The one and only objective of an organization was promoted as wealth-creation, for a fortunate minority. The less fortunate were disregarded in the headlong rush to down-size and to create 'shareholder value'. In the 1990s this philosophy is still alive and kicking, often illustrated in the cruel contrasts between the numbers of redundant staff and the size of top executive bonuses, and highlighted in one corporate scandal after another.

In many countries the gap in wealth between the small minority of super-earners and the great majority of low-paid (often temporary) staff continues to widen. The wealth accumulated by manipulators and gamblers in the fantasy world of finance makes the incomes of most of those who create value from their scientific and technological know-how and those who add value in manufacturing processes look like small change.

All is not well with the world. Periodically, when we learn of a tragedy or scandal on our TV screens and in our newspaper headlines we bemoan for a few days the disintegration of society, and then return forgetfully to our self-centred materialism. For a little while there are calls for a return to values of honesty and respect for human dignity, then the platitudes are packed away until the next painful episode. Is there light and hope in the midst of all this? *Yes, I believe there is*.

Improvement – The darker view

I suspect that pressures for ethical improvement in the business world will continue to build. Many in the 1990s are unlikely to want to change their own ways, especially if it means a slowing in growth of material prosperity; but problems with the behaviour of organizations are easier to attack. Once back in the armchair at home or sitting debating in the pub these can been viewed in a detached manner. 'They' are out there. 'They' are apart from ourselves. It is easy to forget that until 5 o'clock we ourselves were, most of us, part of one of 'Them'. Now that we're outside we can look at 'Them' and criticize, and call for change. Is this an over-cynical view? Maybe. But I believe it to be realistic in many areas of Western society. Large numbers in the populations of advanced technological societies which have abandoned much of traditional personal morality in the name of freedom are likely still to call for many aspects of it in their public institutions and business organizations.

Improvement – The brighter view

This dark view, however, is only a small part of the story. Many are coming to the conclusion that philosophies of amorality and relativism have not been serving Western nations well. They see that the breakdown has to be halted in those frameworks of self-discipline which are necessary for true freedom to flourish. This is too large a subject for this chapter. For the moment I simply want to predict that, without returning to the claustrophobia of so-called 'Victorian values' we will see a continuing move away from the worship of self-interest. As a consequence we will see attempts to impose more effective governance processes within the business world which focus outward on the impact of the corporation on society. Possibly (although I am less optimistic on this score) we will also see a slowdown in the seemingly unstoppable drive to growth and globalization, in which not only individuals but entire communities are all too often treated (whatever the PR) as little better than consumable, and disposable, resources.

I am far from being without hope. I believe that people will act. Whatever my doubts about the morality of modern media systems, which will have become apparent to anyone who has read earlier chapters, they do bring the great benefit of rapid and visible exposure of much wrongdoing where it occurs. Campaigning journalism certainly has its downside, especially where it is more geared to the headline than to the truth, but it seems to me probable that a steady flow of 'human interest' stories associated with corporate misconduct will act to keep up the pressure on organizations to behave better. Transparency will continue to increase, especially in areas of existing public concern such as the general health of the biosphere and oppression of the powerless.

CHANGES IN OUR WORLD

All around the world, people, and the organizations in which they work, are experiencing times of unprecedented change. The causes are to be found within a complex flux of technology and society on a global scale. New ways of living, working and relating are having to be explored and developed. Major areas of change affecting economic life include:

■ The ongoing post-communist transition in many countries, from central planning to various forms of market economy, requiring realignments not only within their own borders but throughout the international trading system.

■ The development of new technologies in fields such as space, advanced materials science, communications, and especially the life sciences, giving rise to many new ethical challenges.

■ The rise of entire new industries based on 'knowledge', shifting the emphasis away from physical to human capital, changing the nature of work and of careers and creating a new genus of jobs which Robert Reich labelled the 'symbolic analyst'.

■ The globalization of business, including the rise of economic power in previously less-developed areas of the globe. Anything can be made anywhere; information can be available in real-time almost anywhere in the world; geographical distance has become in many respects an irrelevance; familiar patterns of organization and interpersonal dynamics are fading into history.

■ Rapidly changing demographic balance, not only between different regions of the world but also within national borders, leading to increasingly elderly populations in the industrialized nations (with corresponding problems of healthcare and pension funding) alongside increasingly young populations in the 'two-thirds world', (with consequent migratory pressures.

■ An increasing lack of a sense of identity as past opponents have faded (for example, it is difficult to view oneself as anti-communist now that communism as a world power is in recession) and as new allegiances and alignments are sought.

■ Widespread concern about the ecological impact of economic growth and the 'carrying capacity' of the total global system.

■ The rise of highly effective ethical campaigning groups on popular issues, many with single-issue focus and little understanding or tolerance of complex dilemmas.

■ A widespread feeling around the world that generally acceptable global ethics and values (to be distinguished clearly from global religion) must be discovered in order to enable peoples of different cultural backgrounds to work together – on all levels, and especially economically and politically.

All of these have massive implications for business life, and indeed can be looked at positively, as they give rise to opportunities for ethical reflection and may therefore lead (if those opportunities are grasped) to improvements in both structures and behaviour.

GEO-POLITICAL DIVIDES AND THE ROLE OF BUSINESS

In the field of geo-political studies many futurists see religious 'walls' replacing those of the communist/capitalist era, with the boundary line between a reviving Islam and the post-Christian West creating multiple flashpoints. The business world is where people of all faiths and cultures come together. Leaders on all sides must face up to the difficult challenge of communicating to their people that to hold dialogue with followers of a different faith or culture around ethical topics of common concern is not the same as compromising the foundational tenets of their belief. For followers of belief systems which are substantially syncretistic this is not too difficult a development. For followers of Islam and of Christianity, both of which combine claims of exclusivity in relation to God and salvation with a corresponding missionary outlook, it is more of a problem.

As has been described in Chapter 19, it has already proved possible to come together and agree on shared business ethics. The relentless expansion of global trade will make such initiatives even more important in the future. Business and other organizational life can only be sustained if built on a foundation of trust. Formal laws of trade are insufficient: *trust* must be developed between peoples with very different worldviews, even when they continue to differ on many other highly important issues. I will continue to be an optimist and expect to see more developments in this direction. Not only is this necessary to support business, but it is a contribution that business can make to world peace.

THE FUTURE ROLE OF FAITH

The impact of strongly believed, committed religion should not be seen as negative, giving rise only to intolerance and division. For very many the pressure for ethical *improvement* will flow from faith – for many, not only in the West, the Christian faith, seeing in Jesus Christ the ultimate model of self-sacrifice given priority over self-interest, and of a resurrection hope even when the future seems dark and impossible.

For others it may flow from other historic religious faiths or from a more general sense of the 'spiritual' in life, of something beyond the immediately visible and physical world of the five senses. I believe that the link between religion and business life will strengthen. It is an interesting phenomenon that in an era when institutionalized religion is, at least in the Western world, losing much of its hold on people, there is in parallel a revival of interest in the impact that faith and spirituality should have on daily living.

The compartmentalized life, in which one's personal faith is boxed up on Sunday evening to keep it well away from the 'real life' of the week and is then brought out again intact, and unchallenged, the following weekend, fails to satisfy millions of people. They are increasingly asking: 'How should my faith affect how I run my business?' 'How should my spiritual values influence the way I deal with my customers, my suppliers, my staff, my banker, my...?' I see this trend continuing, as more and more people search for wholeness and internal consistency in their living.

SOME IMPORTANT CURRENT QUESTIONS

Within business, and its associated academic institutions, there is now increasing speculation about the future of economic life. Thoughtful people around the globe, even many who would not want to be categorized as radical thinkers, are asking questions such as:

- Given that a business requires many different inputs in order to exist and to operate successfully, will it in future be sustainable to view the provider of only one of these (financial capital) as the 'owner' with prior claim over all other stakeholders, especially as knowledge becomes more critical than money within the start-up formula? How should future corporate governance develop?

- To what extent will society require business to measure its success against a broader spectrum of performance criteria, beyond the financial, incorporating standards of behaviour – and not merely as peripheral add-on measures?

- What changes are around the corner in patterns of working, and how will these affect people throughout their careers in different areas of industrial, commercial, domestic and public life?

In addition to social changes there are technological changes, some of which can be predicted, indeed which are already with us, at least as seedlings if not yet as full-grown plants.

Developments in electro-optical technologies, and engineering at the molecular and atomic levels, will revolutionize not only our methods of communication but techniques from manufacturing to medicine and surgery. The biotechnologies, after years of hype, are now about to burst into fruition. Space technology, and at the other extreme exploration and utilization of the deep oceans, are only in their infancies and will bring more change than we can yet envisage.

Business Ethics and Bio-technology

Let us take biotechnology as the source of a few examples. Already for several years ethicists have been at work alongside scientists exploring the moral maze of the human genome project. Bodies such as the Nuffield Foundation have explored the ethical issues in genetic screening, including its implications for the insurance industry and life assurance policies. As techniques of genetic manipulation are developed the debate about patenting of life forms will intensify.

This may all seem rather remote from the life of most businesses, but it is not so. The labelling of foodstuffs containing genetically-engineered components is just one issue. If a tomato contains genetic material from a fish (which already is a reality, aimed at increasing frost-resistance) how will a vegetarian know this? And how is a Muslim or a Jew to know whether vegetable material includes genetic content from animals which are forbidden as food?

Then there is the question of the ownership of life-forms. What impact will there be on a Third World farmer barred from using a proportion of his seed for next year's sowing because it is allegedly the intellectual property of a multinational agribusiness? How many will discover that their new wonder-seed does not in any case grow in the next generation because the plant has been developed to be sterile so as to ensure that next year's seed is paid for? How many such farmers will be driven to join the ranks of the urban poor because they cannot afford the annual royalties demanded?

I do not include these examples as an attack on agribusiness. Far from it. These are complex issues. Past and future research and development have to be paid for by some means. The ethical considerations, however, warrant considerably more public debate, and the implications for GATT and the new World Trade Organization should not be ignored.

Change at the Top

Thinking about the nature and purpose of business and behaviour within and between organizations is not the exclusive domain of idealistic groups of academics and campaigners. It is common also among the ranks of very senior leaders in industry and government. I even heard recently of the chairman of a major transnational taking David Korten's highly provocative book, *When Corporations Rule the World*, with him for summer holiday reading! Projects sponsored by top executives such as the RSA's 'Tomorrow's company' inquiry (and its continuation) in the UK, and similar studies elsewhere, need now to be brought through to reality, to make genuine changes in how businesses function and the criteria against which their performance is assessed.

Ethical Challenges

Just about every profession and field of scientific endeavour now has its ethics committees and enquiries. Independent voluntary organizations of civil society are increasingly aware of how they can work together to greater effect. Most are made up of highly educated, well-informed people who are concerned about the future of humanity, their countries, and the world as a whole.

A prominent example of how such bodies can come together to good effect is 'Real World' in the UK, which describes itself as a 'Coalition of [more than 30] non-governmental organizations committed to raising the importance of environmental sustainability, social justice... and democratic renewal in UK debate.'

Many of the issues with which a coalition of this type will be concerned are not specifically 'business ethics' or even 'organizational ethics.' Having said this, their concerns about the environment, Third World issues, poverty, destructive 'development', and inequality impinge on the business world at many points. I do not necessarily share all the opinions of the Real World coalition; indeed there are probably differences of opinion even among the 30-plus organizations themselves, but I do see this as an indicator of the way things are likely to move in the future – groups of people concerned to build a world in which people really matter, learning how to be more effective together than apart, cutting across traditional political and other divides to meet today's unprecedented challenges.

THREE CAUTIONARY NOTES

It would be remiss of me not to include at this point some words of caution, but I will confine myself to three points: the hazards of seeking international standardization of ethical practice; the risk of business ethics being merely a veneer of respectability spread thinly over an unethical organization; and the dangers of undesirable professionalization in the field.

Rule Books Imposed

It is especially important not to fall into the trap of confusing our own national or industrial etiquette with ethics. Similarly, the fact that we have a law in our country does not make it an ethical imperative for all other countries to have the same law. For example, the United States should take care over attempting to impose precisely its view of what is corrupt, of what constitutes bribery, upon societies which place considerably greater importance on human relationships than does the typical American business person.

The export of codes of business conduct from the country of origin of international companies has long been a difficult enterprise. Too often this is because the codes are more like books of rules than an articulation and exploration of values. A code without clarification of its underlying values can become a straitjacket in an unfamiliar culture. Values, however, can be truly shared and optimum ways of working them out in practice can be developed from country to country in consultation.

Of course, I expect an outcry from people who look for the apparent 'efficiency' of identical action everywhere, but to them I answer: 'What would you rather have? Diversity of immoral behaviour hidden under a veneer of apparent compliance? Or harmony of values applied contextually from society to society?' Do you really expect to be successful in the long term in societies with a culture of gift-giving if you insist that your salesman must not even buy a cup of coffee for a client? Do you really have the moral right to impose your rule about never trading with relatives in an environment where virtually all the business community is interrelated, and for centuries has relied on family trust as its primary defence against being cheated? With such counter-cultural rule books expatriate organizations will never be truly at home, and will either (i) fail, (ii) develop some kind of hypocritical adaptation, or (iii) succeed by virtue of sheer economic power while storing up resentment for the future. Much of this flows from a tendency of many Western business people to confuse rules, which have to be practical, with the underlying values, which should be stable.

Ethics as a Veneer

The danger of creating little more than surface appearances of respectability and compliance is considerable. It leads eventually to disenchantment among staff who know that 'The walk doesn't match the talk.'

As has been mentioned more than once in the course of this book I have a serious concern that some organizations may be treating 'ethics' merely as a matter of public relations, little more than a veneer. As corporate reputation becomes increasingly a vital business asset, to be guarded and developed in an active way, it will become attractive for organizations to participate in conferences, to publish articles in journals, to build ethical content into their advertising. Where this is backed up by reality, it will be an excellent and praiseworthy development. Where it is no more than a cynical exploitation of words and images in order to build wealth on a false foundation it will create serious dangers for the entire business ethics movement, as eventually the mask of expensively proclaimed goodness is penetrated and the underlying rot exposed.

Of course, no organization on the face of the earth is without any flaw. Each is populated by fallible humans, and therefore perfection is unattainable. It will continue to be easy for campaigners to 'explode' and 'expose' company behaviour by exploiting occasional mistakes and isolated weaknesses while choosing to ignore, or relegate to obscure paragraphs, the massive amounts of good, honest work done by these same organizations. Biased investigation is very unlikely to reduce.

Companies will increasingly need to pay close attention to:

- ensuring that when it makes statements about its values and principles it backs them up by action to ensure that they are disseminated throughout the organization;

- monitoring performance and being open about remaining shortcomings and further action being taken in order to improve;

- distinguishing between aspiration and reality, and being honest about this difference;

- learning to communicate its policies and practice effectively, both internally and externally;

- managing 'reputation crises' in ways that will build an ongoing reputation for honesty.

This last requirement is not an easy one. In case of, for example, a serious accident, many will say that faced with the increasing threat of punitive litigation the priority must always be to protect the organization. Certainly the continued prosperous existence of the organization is a valid objective; many stakeholders depend on this; but even in this increasingly litigious world the moral issues must not be ignored.

Considerable further thought is needed in this entire area of corporate image, reputation risk-management, and ethics. I believe that this could be one of the key areas for ethical policy development over the next decade.

The Professionalizing of Business Ethics

Another set of dangers that I foresee are associated with the development of a business ethics 'profession'.

Business ethicists themselves must undergo development. I am not, however, in favour of attempting to develop a pseudo 'profession' of business ethics. Such developments in other fields have frequently been little more than thinly disguised attempts to exclude others who do not conform to their self-stipulated criteria for acceptance as 'true professionals'.

Having said this, there is a need for professional development guidance, and some statement (such as a code of conduct) of the standards of behaviour which can be expected of reputable practitioners.

But what is a 'Business ethicist'? If this book has achieved its purpose the person reading it (yourself) is most probably not a full-time practitioner in this field. You are more likely to be a staff member or manager in an organization, or a self-employed person, who has read parts or all of this book in order to trigger ideas about how to conduct business in a more balanced and ethical manner. You would never consider spending the whole of your time on this topic.

There are, however, people like myself who earn a living by advising companies on a range of subjects within our competence. How many of these are professional ethics advisers? Not many! How many *should* be full-time professional ethics advisers? In my opinion, not many! And this is not a comment on the competence of others but on the desirability of such a development. To isolate this topic from the rest of life as a specialism will, in my judgement, simply lead to the creation of yet another band of detached idealists with little understanding of the business context in which they are operating. If a profession is needed it should be at least as broad as would be implied by Chapter 12 of this book, in which I discussed integrated ethical management.

What *is* needed is a (regularly updated) guide to the body of knowledge which can fairly be expected of a person who purports to advise on a broad spectrum of ethical issues. With this there might be guidance as to how ethical issues can be built into advice in specialist fields. A marketing consultant can then add to his or her body of expertise some competence in analysing and advising on ethical issues in marketing. What I would like to see is a large number of marketing consultants building ethical considerations into their work; similarly, consultants in other fields such as finance, quality, logistics, computing, and etc. What I shudder at is the thought of attempting to license specialist consultants in (say) marketing ethics as a distinct professional field, or even a small army of approved 'general ethics professionals'.

There are enough 'professions' in existence already without adding to their number. The modern craze for establishing a new one every time some new technique or approach is developed, to make certain that the purity of the approach is maintained (that is, to ensure that the organizers' views of such purity is maintained) leads to fragmentation, with dangers of obsolescence and the discrediting of the very concept of profession. It may be argued that auditors of ethical business and social responsibility need standards. There are bodies already in existence for auditors of various kinds. How about developing their role? Why create yet more organizations?

In the field of quality management the idea of a distinct breed of people known as 'quality managers' is rapidly becoming obsolete. Why? Because quality is something to be built into everything we do, and not an area of expertise for a select few. Surely ethics is a similar case. A defined body of knowledge, and a code of conduct for the few people working most of their time with it? Yes! But a 'profession'? No!

The debate continues. My views may eventually be changed by the force of solid argument. Of one thing I am sure: these three cautions must not be ignored.

WORKING ON THE ORGANIZATION

Finally, in your organization, what should be the ethical change agenda for the next decade as we enter the 21st century? Each of the following points has already been covered in previous chapters and I do not intend to repeat much detail here, but will conclude with a fourfold programme which can be expanded by revisiting earlier chapters.

1. *Re-invent your organization.* Consider carefully what should be its foundation values for the next decade and more, exploring not only what are its rights to demand of others, but what are its corporate responsibilities to all stakeholders. Associated with this, develop innovative new measures of performance, going beyond the traditional counts and ratios of money and considering the interests of all upon whom it has an impact in its working life. Involve your bright young people as well as the mature, even elderly, 'leadership' in thinking this through. Channel great energies into promoting your new vision to all your stakeholders, especially any who might initially seek to hold you back. Consider what it all

means for how you are organized, not only in formal structural terms but in the interpersonal processes by which people work together, and through which decisions are made.

2. *Experiment with new approaches to top-level guidance and governance* of the organization. Make sure that you do not lose sight of the fact that in order to transform into something new you must first of all survive the metamorphosis; don't allow woolly thinking; don't allow an over-concentration on experimentation and change to cause you to lose control of the critical determinants of survival. Be prepared for a long haul and for disappointments along the way. Do not listen to enthusiasts who believe all you need to do is to flick a switch. Ignore mechanics who tell you that this is just about new rules and formal paperwork. Support your governance system by regular and challenging audits.

3. *Build a values-driven organization.* Articulate your values. Publicize them. Constantly repeat them. Revisit them annually. Consider whether they're expressed in the best way. Ask whether there is some important value that you've missed in the past. Don't be afraid to learn, to adapt, to retrench if necessary.

4. *Incorporate the values into all decision processes* at all levels, in all areas and aspects of the organization. Treat compliance with the non-financial values as being of at least equal importance to those concerned with money. Remember, the aim is not to oust money and sound financial thinking from the business – that will be a sure road to ruin. It is to integrate financial criteria and others of equal, and at times even greater, importance which have often been relegated to a lesser status in the past.

Finally, this road will be hard. If you've got it anything like right in ten years' time you will have done well.

Useful References

David Korten (1995) *When Corporations Rule the World*, Earthscan, London.

Index